PASSENGER 19C

A Memoir of Survival

Margo E. Siple

ISBN 978-1-63961-070-9 (paperback)
ISBN 978-1-63961-072-3 (hardcover)
ISBN 978-1-63961-071-6 (digital)

Christian Faith Publishing
832 Park Avenue
Meadville, PA 16335
www.christianfaithpublishing.com

Printed in the United States of America

To my children, Bryson and Molly, for
giving me something to live for.
To my parents, Rip and Ruth, and my sister
Babette, for always being there for me.
To my husband, Kelly, my "personal pilot"
for encouraging me to tell my story.
To everyone in the "232 Family"

Contents

Acknowledgments

Thank you to all of my family, friends, and professionals
that helped me process my life after the crash.
Thank you to Captain Al Haynes and his amazing airline
crew. Thank you to Jerry Schemmel, Garry Priest, Rod Vetter,
Oprah, Dr. Bob Boyle, *the Rocky Mountain News*, and *the
Littleton Independent*. I appreciate all of the endless resources
that were provided via books, newspapers, and interviews.
A special thanks to Sioux City and all of the personnel that
were on duty that day: the medical staff at Marian Health
Center and St. Luke's Hospital, Sioux City Gateway Airport,
Sioux City Fire, Police and Emergency Medical Service
Departments, Sioux City officials, Briar Cliff College, and the
Iowa Air National Guard's 185th Tactical Fighter Group.

Introduction

On July 19, 1989, I was the passenger in seat 19-C, aboard United Flight 232, which crash-landed in a Sioux City, Iowa, cornfield after losing all hydraulics. Flight 232 was one of the fifth deadliest airline crashes involving a DC-10. Among the 296 souls on board, 112 perished, including 1 airline attendant; 172 passengers survived, as well as 3 pilots and 7 flight attendants. Many of the 184 people who survived were seriously injured, while very few passengers walked away under their own power. I was one of the few who walked away without a scratch. Although there were many years of emotional healing afterward, I was able to put my life back together and reflect on this life-changing event. Survivor's guilt, processing, healing, moving on. These affect the lives of the survivors and the families of those who perished. Many questions of why this happened will never be answered. Only after many years did I stop asking the question of "why did I survive, and others die?" I will always be processing, healing, and moving on, but I am at the point in my life now that I can talk about and remember that fateful day without having any survivor's guilt. Even though it is inevitable that airline crashes will continue to happen, it is known that currently, no commercial aircraft is built with the hydraulic design that the DC-10 had. The specific incident with regards to the loss of all hydraulics should not happen again. As with any devastating incident, lessons are learned.

Flight 232

Dear Lord,

Where do I begin
To express what words can't say
Or share with you the thoughts
Going through my mind today
I close my eyes and wonder
If I am living proof
To those who say you saved me
And make it sound so true
But if, my Lord, you saved me
There's something I have missed
For with my eyes I've seen
Those you didn't bless
It's hard for me to understand
The logic that you'd use
To save the gift of life, and yet
For only those you choose

—Garry Priest

I've never met a strong person with an easy past.

—Unknown

❖ Have God in your life
❖ Never take anything for granted
❖ Every day, tell your family and children that you love them
—Advice from a loved one

There are seven large boulders leading to the lower plaza of the memorial. Each one of them has a cast brass plaque with a moving quote about the people who aided in the effort or words spoken by rescuers themselves.

- ❖ "There are certain moments in life you simply have to enter..."
- ❖ "Remember, I love you... I care about you..."
- ❖ "There was always someone there."
- ❖ "I didn't save him... God saved the child. I just carried him, sir."
- ❖ "There was no hesitation, we did what we had to do."
- ❖ "Let no one go unmentioned. Yet, once again, we say, we're very proud of Siouxland and all who helped that day."
- ❖ "The whole community of Sioux City reached inside itself and found resources it didn't know it had...found that this is who we really are."

*Three-year-old Spencer Bailey and Lt. Col. Dennis Nielsen of the
Iowa Air National Guard's 185th Tactical Fighter Group.*

Rocky Mountain News

The picture that appeared in newspapers around the world: Air National Guard Col. Dennis Nielsen carrying Spencer Bailey from the wreckage of United Airlines Flight 232.

This is the iconic picture that inspired the permanent memorial of Flight 232 by artist Dale Lamphere.

****

Statistics (Some of these are referenced from Wikipedia*)*

July 19, 1989: United Airlines Flight 232, a sixteen-year-old McDonnell Douglas DC-10, registered as N1819U, en route from Denver Stapleton International Airport to Chicago O'Hare International Airport. It was "Children's Day" and child tickets were

14

only one cent. There were 285 passengers; 52 of which were children (including 8 infants and 4 lap); and 11 crew. A total of 296 souls on board.

After a short delay, which was due to an electrical problem, the plane took off at 1:09 p.m. Mountain time zone; (2:09 p.m. Central time zone). One hour and seven minutes after taking off, the explosion was heard (2:16 p.m. Mtn. and 3:16 p.m. Central). Forty-four minutes later, the plane impacted (3:00 p.m. Mtn. and 4:00 p.m. Central).

(Please note that there were roughly forty to forty-four minutes from the sound of the explosion until the time the actual crash took place. Different references refer to these as forty or forty-four minutes.)

The jetliner was flying a routine flight to Philadelphia, with a layover in Chicago at thirty-seven thousand feet, over Alta, Iowa, when there was a very loud, sudden explosion, as if a bomb had gone off inside the plane. Little did those 296 souls on board know that there was only forty-four minutes left to decide their fate. Some would die, some would be seriously wounded, and some would walk away under their own power after the plane crashed.

The passenger fatality and survivor numbers fluctuate in various articles and write-ups. The final numbers that were recorded in Wikipedia are as follows:

296 Occupants
285 Passengers
11 Crew
172 Injuries
184 Survivors
112 Fatalities

The explosion heard was the number 2 engine. The cause was by an undetected flaw in the 290-pound titanium metal disk that forms the hub of the engine's fan blade assembly. Investigation and metallurgy tests showed that the metal was unevenly forged, leaving a small weak spot in the vanadium-titanium metal. Over the years, the weak section went undetected, and the metal became fatigued. After the engine exploded, shards of metal from pieces of the engine peppered the tail section, severing all three of the plane's hydraulic lines. Without hydraulic lines, the plane is virtuously lifeless and uncontrollable. The system acts as the plane's "muscles," enabling the pilots to control and operate the wing flaps and many other crucial flight systems.

The plane was banking to the right. If not corrected, it would become inverted and unrecoverable, falling and smashing into the earth who-knows-where. Everything and everyone would be disintegrated. "An impossible landing." "The odds of all three hydraulic systems failing simultaneously had previously been calculated as high as a billion to one" (from Wikipedia).

Denny Fitch, an off-duty training check airman, was a passenger on board Flight 232. After he realized that the plane was having difficulty flying, he offered his aid to help in the cockpit. Captain Haynes asked him to manipulate the flight controls to control pitch and roll. While on his knees, he had to use both hands to manipulate the throttles because the numbers 1 and 3 thrust levers could not be used symmetrically.

With no hydraulics, the crew were only able to make right-hand turns. However, they needed to try a left-hand turn to reach Sioux City, where they had been cleared for an emergency landing. Captain Haynes was ready to "ditch" and put it down wherever it happened to be, but with the efforts of all in the cockpit, they were eventually able to complete two slow right turns, all the while descending. These right turns took the plane southbound. Fitch was able to maneuver a left turn and then flew a 360, which he was able to stop just as the airport lay ahead of them (see flight path of 232). By increasing and decreasing power to its wing engines, Captain Haynes was able to steer the plane, lining it up on a closed 6,888-foot-long runway. Runway 22.

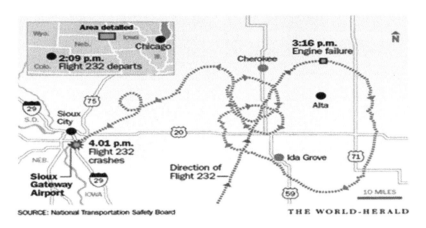

Flight path of 232 from point of engine failure

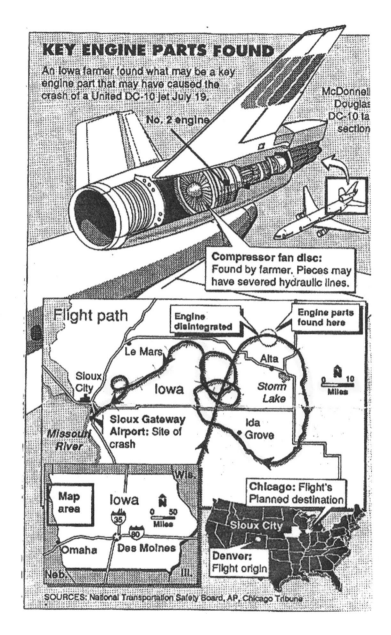

KEY ENGINE PARTS FOUND

An Iowa farmer found what may be a key engine part that may have caused the crash of a United DC-10 jet July 19.

McDonnell Douglas DC-10 tail section

No. 2 engine

Compressor fan disc: Found by farmer. Pieces may have severed hydraulic lines.

Flight path

Engine disintegrated

Engine parts found here

Le Mars

Alta

Sioux City

Iowa

Storm Lake

0   10
Miles

Sioux Gateway Airport: Site of crash

Ida Grove

Missouri River

Wis.

Map area

Iowa

0   50
Miles

35

80

Chicago: Flight's Planned destination

Sioux City

Omaha

Des Moines

Denver: Flight origin

Neb.

Ill.

SOURCES: National Transportation Safety Board, AP, Chicago Tribune

On final descent, the aircraft was going 240 knots and sinking at 1,850 feet per minute upon approach. A safe and regular landing for this type of aircraft would require a speed of 140 knots and descend 300 feet per minute. Going 100 knots faster than a regular landing and sinking fast was horrifying.

After reconstructions of the accident and thirty testing attempts on flight simulators that were ran in Dallas and Denver using United flight crews, there were no successful landings. The alternate thrusting of the engines caused the plane to "porpoise." The pilot had no control of the ailerons, which control the roll rate (left and right movement) and no control of the elevators, which control the pitch (nose up and down). It was reported that this is not a trainable maneuver. The event involved too many factors to be practical.

> Of the 296 passengers and crew on board, 112 died during the accident, while 184 people survived. The crash was the fifth deadliest one involving the DC-10. Despite the deaths, the accident is considered a prime example of successful *crew resource management* because of the considerable number of survivors and the manner in which the flight crew handled the emergency and landed the airplane without conventional control. While some level of control was possible, no precision could be achieved, and a landing under these conditions was stated to be "a highly random event." The NTSB further noted that "under the circumstances the UAL flight crew performance was highly commendable and greatly exceeded reasonable expectations." (Wikipedia)

Because of these statistics and the multitude of the crash, I think of it as one of the worst yet most successful disasters in aviation.

Prologue

The silence that settled over us was like that of fresh, light falling snow. A reprieve in which minutes ticked by where it seemed like everybody was holding their breath and waiting for the next onslaught of terror to strike us. Like the eye of a hurricane, we were only safe for a little while, as all around us, total catastrophe was unfolding. There was still more of the storm to come. Only if we began moving would we be able to outrun it, or so we thought.

Like all stories that involve more than one person's memory, they are all different. Each person sees the same thing in a unique perspective and recalls it in a separate way. When someone remarks on what a dreadful day they are having, I want to tell them the story about the worst day of my life. Depending upon the multitude of their problem, after they have explained what is so frustrating about their dreadful day, I simply tell them, "You'll get through it. This day will end, and when you wake up tomorrow morning, it will seem trivial. I have bad days too, but they all seem very moderate to what I consider one of the worst days in history and in my life. All of the frustrating, horrible days I've had don't even come close to equaling the one certain day in my memory."

These are the thoughts and the outlook on life that I hold in my heart and my mind every day. These thoughts, along with a lot of faith, strength, and prayer, are what help me get through the most difficult and adverse times in my life.

First Dream

The maiden flight of the new glass bottom airplane was going smoothly. What a beautiful sight to witness the tops of the tall blue spruce, majestic evergreens, and fluttering aspen trees. To be able to spot bird nests snuggled among the long green branches and feel like the elite group of species that can only see from this point of view was a once-in-a-lifetime event! The sense of really feeling like a bird and being able to fly when and where you wanted, to soar or to dive and float on the wind was a dream come true! This event was made especially wonderful with the presence of my children and sister. We were on the maiden flight of the first glass bottom plane. How far technology had advanced to be able to create, build, and fly an aircraft such as this! It was twice as remarkable to be able to fly low enough to feel like you had become one with the earth and the landscape you were flying over. My children were young at the time and extremely excited to be a part of this. This was history in the making. An event that would be talked about for years and years to come.

Until things started to go wrong.

Suddenly, the trees seemed to race up to meet the bottom of the plane. The ground was close enough to see every outline, color, shape, and features of its rocks, dirt, weeds, and flowers. We were guaranteed to feel close to the earth, but this seemed a little too close. Before we knew it, the bottom of the plane kissed the earth, and we were sent cartwheeling through trees, past rocks and through water until we ended up in a broken heap of debris and broken glass in the middle of a cornfield. The air was alive with the roaring sound of fire and the feel of the smothering heat of that fire. There were cries of fear and anguish from some of the people that had been on board the airplane. There was also the distinct and unforgettable smell of burning trees, grass, oil, fuel, and one new smell that I will never forget and later identify as that of burning human flesh.

Through the smoke and haze of the fire and mayhem, I spotted my sister holding my son, Bryson. They seemed dazed but unhurt. "Where is Molly?" I asked her in a frantic voice.

"I don't know where she is. She flew out of my arms on impact!" she replied.

It was during this frantic time of trying to find my daughter, with the crushed, burning plane looming in front of me, and calling out her name, that I awoke from the most terrifying dream I had had since the real plane crash I had recently been in.

1

DEALING WITH TRAUMA

My story began on July 19, 1989.

Every day of our lives, we should be prepared for whatever hand life deals us, but most often, we are not. I had been dealt about three difficult hands up to my thirty-first year; all of them life-threatening and life-changing. Each situation was traumatic, but none of them could compare to the incident that happened on a beautiful summer day, July 19, 1989. The crash of United Airlines Flight 232, in Sioux City, Iowa, changed thousands of lives that day, not just my own.

Some stories come from our imagination, some from our dreams, and some from real life encounters. Everybody has their own unique life story, including major events, traumatic events, or happy events to tell. It is whether they choose to tell them and how they tell them that make the difference.

Like a game of dominos, one event connects with another, leading you on the path of your life, and along the way, you are asked to make decisions and to approach encounters that are out of your control. No matter how many years have passed since that fateful day, when people learn of my survival of one of the world's major airplane crashes, they are very intrigued to hear my story. Questions of "how did you survive?", "how did you feel during the whole thing?", "what did you see?" are always asked. Some people who are unwilling to believe that miracles do happen look at me as if I were a walking, talking, living ghost.

When I replay the events and important parts of my life leading up to that day, I can only conclude that life is very fragile as well as unpredictable. Every day, every minute, every event leads us to the next until we can reflect and remember what's been, but never of what's to become.

For as long as I can remember, I have always been a nature lover. Whether it was reading about it in books and magazines, or watching documentaries on the television, or simply witnessing it myself, I always found solitude in the wonders of Mother Nature. To see the sky, mountains, rivers, flowers, trees, grass, birds, various species of animals, and all of Mother Nature coming alive in the spring has always been a miracle to me as well as the wonders of the human life. Giving birth and witnessing a new life begin is the ultimate miracle that we as female human beings have been blessed with. I do know that miracles do happen. I am one. "I feel like I'm a miracle." This is the quotation on a treasured pin I received from St. Luke's Hospital in Sioux City, Iowa. I carry it everywhere, as it is as much a part of me as one of my limbs. There are miracles all around us every day of our lives, but unfortunately, a lot of us do not realize them or see them. The day of July 19, 1989 and the fateful crash of United Airlines Flight 232 was a miracle that has become infamous all over the world.

When I was still in my early twenties, I went back to work after giving birth to my first child, my son Bryson. After he was about one year old, I put my son in day care and went to work for a savings and loan bank in downtown Denver, Colorado. I would catch the public bus and ride it from Golden, Colorado, where I lived at the time, to downtown Denver. It was a small branch, and there were only two tellers working there at one time.

One morning, just days before my birthday, I ended up working alone for a few hours. I remember watching this person walking back and forth in front of the bank door. My senses were heightened, as it was an odd show of behavior. Then this person did come through the door, and I saw that it was a young male, medium height with a hoodie on. As I was standing behind the teller counter, he approached me with his hand in his right pocket. There was an object in the pocket pointed straight at me. He looked me in the eye and demanded the money that was in my teller drawer. As nervous as I was, I remembered to pull the silent alarm that was located under the teller counter before giving him all the cash (about $10,000) that was in my drawer. He grabbed the cash from me and ran out the front door.

Activation of the alarm was supposed to set the security cameras in action. However, after the police came and I looked at some mug shots, it was discovered that there was no film in the cameras! The culprit was never caught.

I was relieved of my duties that day and sent home early. All I wanted to do was pick up my son from day care, go home, and curl up in bed. I recall that the reality of the bank robbery didn't really hit me until I was home. My thoughts ran with the truth that I may never have seen my son again, or had another birthday, if the bank robber had decided to shoot me. Whether there was a weapon in his pocket or not was unknown. My life had been threatened, and I could only imagine the other things that he could have done to me with us being the only two people inside the bank at the time. I did not return to work at the bank. There was not going to be any professional security to guard the branch. My life was more important. I decided I was going to stay at home with my young son.

A couple of years after that, I gave birth to my daughter Molly. Her birth was another life-threatening episode in my young life.

I had had a full term and normal pregnancy with Bryson, but my second pregnancy was difficult and life-threatening. The day before I had to have an emergency C-section was spent in the mountains on a fishing trip. Bryson's father and I had taken him up to the beautiful Colorado mountains to go fishing. Early June in Colorado is so beautiful! Everything is blooming and waking up from a long winter's sleep. Bryson was three at the time and enjoyed the outdoors as much as we did. I spent the day in some discomfort, but didn't think much about it, as I had had quite a few Braxton-Hicks contractions throughout my six-month term. However, as the day went on, I became very fatigued, with a bad backache.

By the time we got home in the early evening, I was in excruciating pain all throughout my midsection and back. After putting a tired and sleepy child to bed, I tried to lie down and get some sleep also. After about an hour of tossing and turning, I realized that the pain was going to keep me from getting any sleep that night. I can best describe the pain as numerous sharp knives being poked into my abdomen and back, noticeable swelling of my ankles and legs; nothing like Braxton-Hicks contractions. This pain was something entirely different and scary. After waiting a couple of hours to see if the pain would recede (which it did not) we decided to go to the emergency room.

Bryson had stated during my whole pregnancy that he wanted a baby sister, and we wanted to give him one, only not this early in my pregnancy! While I lay on a bed in the emergency room, my husband called his parents to ask them if they could pick up Bryson and watch him until we knew what was going on. After an exceptionally long wait in fear and horrible pain, I finally saw a doctor. Then a specialist was called, in which my condition and signs were described to him, and he ordered an emergency C-section. I had developed preeclampsia.

Preeclampsia is a disorder of pregnancy characterized by the onset of high blood pressure and often a significant amount of protein in urine. When it arises, the condition begins after twenty weeks of pregnancy. In severe disease, there may be red blood cell breakdown, a low blood platelet count, impaired liver function, kidney dysfunction, swelling, shortness of breath due to fluid in the lungs, or visual disturbances. Preeclampsia increases the risk of poor outcomes for both the mother and the baby. If left untreated, it may result in seizures, at which point it is known as eclampsia.

I was then rushed to surgery. When I awoke, I hadn't realized what had happened but was then told by a nurse that they had to take the baby and that she was small. "I need to see my baby. Please let me see my baby!" I was very frightened and confused when they told me that she would be transported to Fitzsimmons Hospital in Aurora, Colorado, because there were no beds available in the neonatal unit at the hospital we were at.

"She weighs two pounds, half ounce and is very small and needs exceptional care," the nurse told me. "We will bring her in so you can see her before we transport her."

When I did finally get to see "Molly," the first thought that went through my mind was that I had given birth to a bird. Of course, I was still drugged from the surgery, but she did look like a newborn bird when they are first hatched. They are so tiny and delicate, their skin is transparent, and you can see the veins running through their body. That was the first look I had of my new baby girl.

After falling back into a drug-induced sleep, I woke again to find my parents sitting anxiously by my bed. Their concern for my well-being was written all over their faces. As always, being wonderful parents, they have always been there for my sister and me through good times and bad. They have never faltered in their strength or faith through all the trials of our lives. As I was still very tired and confused, I asked them what all the tubes and bags were that I was hooked up to. "You needed a blood transfusion, and they are watching for signs of any kidney problems that might occur due to the pregnancy," my father told me. He did not elaborate on my delicate state of illness, and only later did I find out that my blood platelets needed replacement and that my kidneys could fail, leading to dialysis. Later, my father also told me that I had been at the brink of death, as my body was starting to shut down. While I was struggling to survive for myself and my baby, he had gone to the hospital chapel, gotten down on his knees, and prayed for both of us, for our survival and future health.

The doctors told me that I should not have any more children, as my body would not be able to survive it, therefore the baby would not either. I had my two children that I had wanted and prayed for: a son and a daughter. I needed no further orders.

After waking and becoming lucid, I yearned to see Molly and be with her, but they had already transported her to Fitzsimmons Hospital (about fifteen miles away), and I was too sick to leave the hospital. During the three days I was in the hospital, my kidneys started functioning, and my blood returned to normal, so I was finally discharged from the hospital. Those three days without being able to see Molly were the longest days of my life! I would call Fitzsimmons at least three or four times a day to check up on her. I was always told that she was doing fine but still extremely sick. As soon as I was dismissed from the hospital, the first stop we made was at Fitzsimmons to see her. Bryson was with us, and he could hardly wait to see his baby sister.

After three months of visiting Molly at Fitzsimmons Hospital every day, we finally were able to bring her home. It was around her original due date, which was mid-September, if she had been full term. She weighed only five pounds and was on oxygen 24-7. She did have some serious problems while she was hospitalized, which included numerous blood gas tests and a skin and blood staph infection. However, she fought hard and survived all of this and is a survivor to this day.

I had to buy doll clothes for her. She was still so small and delicate. Diapers for premature babies had to be special ordered. Being on oxygen 24-7 required a large oxygen tank to stand by her crib and a long oxygen tube attached to her so that I could carry her as I moved around the house. I would wake up every hour on the hour at night to check on her to make sure she was breathing. During the day, she was with me every moment. We didn't leave the house much then except for numerous doctor visits, and when we did, it was necessary to hook her up to a portable oxygen tank for transporting. For three months, this became our normal life. It was a stressful time but also a unique, sensitive time in which I bonded with Molly outside the womb.

She has grown into a wonderful woman and is a caregiver herself. She is one of the miracles in my life.

2

DAY IN HISTORY

On July 19, 1989, no one could foresee what was to come, and certainly we couldn't predict the results. The day would become one big piece of a puzzle; the rest we had to put together ourselves, if we survived long enough to do so.

I woke early on the morning of July 19, 1989 with the excited anticipation of traveling on a business trip to Chicago, a city I had heard so much about and had only glimpsed once on a previous visit. I was looking forward to another visit, not even dreaming that I would become more familiar with God and the cornfields of Sioux City, Iowa, on that day, instead of the city of Chicago.

Bryson and Molly are my two beautiful children. In 1989, Bryson was ten years old, and Molly was seven. They were going to Lakeside amusement park with their father on this sunny, warm summer day and were excited at the prospect of riding the roller coaster and all the other exciting, breathtaking rides they were going to go on. I was going to take my own roller coaster ride through an Iowa cornfield that day. I just did not know it.

After hugging my children Bryson and Molly, and telling them I loved them, I drove my usual route to work. I was currently working for a regional office of a large life insurance company and had the most wonderful boss, one of those that only come along once in a lifetime. Bill hired me one year earlier as his administrative assistant, knowing that I knew nothing about life insurance. He had enough faith and trust in me to know that I would learn quickly. Our personalities "clicked," and we had a wonderful rapport that enabled us to work well together. He was a regional vice president and traveled often. It was common for him to fly a couple of times a week. I always took care of his travel arrangements as well as my own. Bill and I were supposed to fly together to Chicago that day in first class. Rarely do I get to fly in first class, so I was disappointed when his plans changed, and he told me that he had another destination that he was traveling to on that day. With the sudden change of plans on the morning of July 19, I walked down the hall to the travel agency and spoke to Ellen.

"I'm going to move your seat assignment to one over the wing. It's safer over the wing," she said.

"Sure, that's fine with me," I said.

"Have a safe trip," she replied.

Little did I know that my life and fate had just been altered by this change of my seat in the plane. (At least 90 percent of the people seated in first class died that day.) Thanking her and accepting my ticket, I stopped by my friend Sandy's office on the way back to my own office to say goodbye, as I would be gone for a few days.

I still remember the first time Sandy and I met while working in the same office building. We ran into each other in the hallway one day.

"You look very familiar," she said. "Where did you go to high school?"

I graduated from Columbine High School, and she graduated from Green Mountain High School, but as it turned out, we went to Bear Creek, the same high school during our sophomore year. We never knew each other, but she remembered seeing my face now and then in the hallways. Our friendship took a sudden strong hold. It is still strong today. We have seen each other through a lot of adversities—everything from work, children, husbands (and ex-husbands), divorce, boyfriends, shared secrets, and financial problems. We also enjoyed some fun and carefree adventures together. Our offices were only a couple of doors away from each other, which made those times, when a helping hand, a sympathetic ear, or just an invitation for lunch, very convenient. Currently, we were both going through a difficult, failing marriage. We each had two children to think about raising and unanswered questions if we became single mothers. The answer to these questions came much sooner for me than I expected.

At the airport, I noticed that there were two different flights to Chicago leaving at about the same time. I remember following an airline attendant to the same gate to board Flight 232. She had beautiful, stunning, long red hair with a large navy-blue bow fixed at the back of her head. She was slender and exceptionally beautiful and looked to be in her early twenties. Her name was Rene Louise LeBeau. Later, it was hard to realize that she had had only about two more hours to live before her young life would end in an instant.

As is usual in everyday situations, we do not recall the exact sights, sounds, colors, feelings, or importance of that time until forced to. However, today, after many years of healing, I can recall the exact faces and my own thoughts and feelings while waiting to board United Flight 232 to Chicago. Of the faces that I can recall clearly, each have a name and a story behind them.

Jerry Schemmel, Jay Ramsdale, Garry Priest, Rod Vetter, and Ron Sheldon. Each of these strangers were on the same fateful flight. I did not know any of them that morning. However, in the days following the crash, we were able to share our stories with each other, except for Jay Ramsdale, who was not among the fortunate ones to survive. Sometimes, by observing their appearance and watching a person's expression and their body language, you can perceive a person's state of mind. I recall watching Jerry and Jay at the check-in counter, as they both seemed agitated. I later learned that they were business partners and best friends, and both had been trying since earlier that morning to get a flight to Chicago. For several reasons, each of them was on standby, and with each attempt, they had either been bumped from a flight or it had been cancelled. They were finally able to board United 232 together but were assigned seats that were not even close to each other.

I recall boarding the plane behind Garry, as he stood out, being well over six-feet tall, young, and good-looking. Rod and Ron were the gentlemen who were seated to the right of me in the same row. My seat was in row 19, seat C, which was the beginning of the middle row. Rod was in seat D, and Ron was in seat E. Rod was already in his seat when I approached. He took one look at the expression of dismay on my face, as I was trying to figure out how to fit my carry-on luggage among all the other luggage already stored in the overhead bin.

"Would you like help with that?" he asked.

"Yes, thank you," I replied.

He did find a place for my luggage, and we started a casual conversation as we were preparing for takeoff. I usually do not strike up conversations with fellow passengers on airplanes, but Rod and Ron were two nice men who made conversation easy, and I felt myself responding and taking part in the conversation.

Before takeoff, as the airline attendants were presenting the pre-flight instructions, they emphasized that there were many children on the flight, as there was a special promotion going on. There were also many families on board. The safety of all the passengers, especially the small children and babies that were being held in their parent's lap, was especially important.

Since the crash, Jan Brown, the senior airline attendant, has become an advocate for children that have no assigned seat and, therefore, only held in a parent's lap, with no safety restraint.

In the brief time we talked before the explosion on the plane, I found out that Rod lived in Chicago but was originally from Loveland, Colorado. He had been a Navy pilot, loved to golf and owned his own business. I did not get as familiar with Ron, as he was sitting on the opposite side of Rod, but I do remember that he had a family and was also traveling on business. I usually do not even give my name when traveling, but Rod and Ron eventually knew my name, my children's names, where I lived and worked, and what book I was currently reading, all within one hour of the flight.

If you have ever heard a shot gun or cannon go off suddenly and without warning right next to you, you will never forget the loud deafening noise to your ears, or the way it makes your heart hammer in your chest and at the same time feel like it is in your throat. The sudden rush of adrenaline caused from fear and surprise crawls throughout your bloodstream like a giant, slow, poisonous snake. It takes over your entire body and leaves you trembling. This was what occurred while the crew and passengers were enjoying their lunch. They served chicken fingers for lunch, and to this day, I can never eat chicken fingers without reliving that moment of fear after hearing the blast.

We were thirty-seven thousand feet in the air, aboard a maximum-loaded, 290-ton, DC-10 airplane when the explosion occurred. I remember looking at Rod with a look of confusion and incomprehension on my face. He in turn looked at me with the same expression.

"What was that?" were the words and voices of not just myself and Rod, but of fellow passengers around me. There was not any mass confusion or panic, just worry written on everyone's face. The people who were in their seats remained so, and those who were not in their seats walked quickly back to them and sat down (hopefully securing their seat belts).

The plane did not seem to be flying as smoothly as it had been. Looks of confusion and fear were now clear on surrounding passengers' faces. Even though it felt like the plane was going in a nose-dive, I later learned that it climbed and almost went belly-up. Various thoughts and memories flashed through my mind at this time. I pictured the plane spiraling down nose first into an unrecoverable spin, stopping only when the ground came up to meet it. *It will be over quickly if it happens that way*, I thought. I pictured my children growing up without me. Above anything else, I just could not accept the fact that it was possible that I would not be alive to watch my children grow up. I thanked God that they were not on the plane with me, as my worst nightmare has always been the chance that I would outlive my children.

Making sure my seat belt was as secure and tight as I could make it, I tried to take my mind off the shuddering and the loud noise that the plane was making. As always, when I become nervous, my bladder will feel like it is about to explode. Eventually, summoning up the courage, I unbuckled my seat belt and slowly made my way to the bathroom. I had to hold onto the end of the seat at each aisle, as it was extremely hard to keep my balance. In the restroom, I asked myself, "Are you crazy? Something could happen to this plane this instant, and I'll be totally unprepared and vulnerable." I hurriedly made my way back to my seat as best as I could, noticing that one woman was crawling on her hands and knees down the aisle; the shuddering and bucking of the plane was so wild.

After sitting down and securing my seat belt again, I received some encouraging words from Rod. He told me that he had been a Navy pilot and that hopefully it was just the loss of an engine, and if so, that things would be all right, as commercial planes can fly on two engines. I clung to his words and faith, hoping and praying for the best outcome. We noticed a man that looked official walking up and down the aisle. He headed to the rear of the plane and returned a few minutes later. We saw him doing this a couple of times. During this forty-minute period, I was trying to keep up a light conversation with Rod to keep my mind off the trouble we might be in. However, my mind was racing back into the past, as well as ahead into the future. I was recalling various important memories and thinking of "what if" scenarios of things to come, depending upon the results of our current situation. I knew I needed to be strong. Not only for myself, but for my fellow passengers (if any help would be needed) and for my family. I have always dealt with traumatic situations better than the normal day-to-day trials and challenges. The everyday trials and challenges tend to become mundane, but the sudden traumatic events I respond to in a separate way. This is the only logic I can attribute to my reactions and the actions I took after the plane crashed.

I lost all interest in the book I was reading. (I did not recover that book after the crash, but I bought another copy and did eventually finish it.) The lunch of chicken fingers that had been served earlier was also forgotten. (It took me years afterward to be able to eat chicken fingers again and not always associate them with doom.) The airline attendants were unhurriedly, but authoritatively, gathering up the uneaten meals. I anxiously waited for any update from the captain over the intercom. I felt that if he was still communicating with us, then things were going to be all right. During the forty minutes since the explosion and before the crash, he had been on the intercom a couple of times. His voice was always reassuring and calm. "This is Captain Haynes." He went on to explain that we had experienced a problem with the number 2 engine and that it would have to be shut down. He reassured us that the DC-10 was able to fly without it and that the plane can fly with the two remaining engines. However, this would cause us to be a little late in arriving in Chicago.

Later, again, his calm but commanding voice came over the intercom into the cabin. This time, he announced that the explosion had also damaged the rear of the plane and that he and the crew were working together to get it under control. The flight attendants were then instructed to prepare for an emergency landing, and they set about doing this in a very precise, professional way. We, the passengers, were told not to leave our seats under any circumstance. We were instructed to locate the nearest emergency exit. They demonstrated the two separate ways in which to brace ourselves for the landing when the command came. One was to lean forward, grasp our ankles, and put our head between our knees if it were physically possible. The other way was to cross our arms, grasp the top of the seat in front of us, and burrow our head into our arms. After landing, we were to leave all purses, briefcases, and any other carry-on luggage on the plane, continue to the nearest exit and, by crossing our arms over our chest and in a sitting position, slide down the emergency chute that would deploy automatically.

There seemed to be a lot of talking, whispering, and soft crying going on around me. I was thinking about my children, thanking God that they were not with me on this plane and praying that I might live to see them again. A few memories of their growing up played themselves out behind my closed eyes. Like a movie trailer that shows a little bit of each scene all within a few minutes, I watched my children grow from when they were infants up to their current ages of ten and seven. I thought about the rest of my family and wondered how they would react to the news of my outcome, whatever that would be. There was not a lot of time to reminisce about my life with my wonderful family, even though it seemed like an eternity that we were stalled in midair on a crippled plane between death and doom or survival and living. I was just thankful that none of my family were on the plane with me.

Once again, Captain Hayne's voice came on the intercom. He told us that we would not be reaching Chicago and would have to make an emergency landing in Sioux City, Iowa. He said, "I'm not going to kid you," and he warned us that the landing was going to be "very, very rough" and to follow all emergency procedures once the plane was on the ground. I was close to one of the emergency exits. My first thought was of having to go down the emergency slide after it was deployed. *It could be exciting,* I thought. Little did I know that I would not be "sliding" down the emergency chute at all but crawling my way through a hot, fiercely burning fuselage with my new friend Rod's voice the only thing to guide me. Earlier, while Rod and I were talking, he had promised to buy me a drink after we landed. He did not get to buy me that drink until years later.

Captain Haynes told us that his command before the emergency landing would be "brace, brace, brace." At that command, we were to assume the crash position which we had been earlier instructed on. Being quite flexible, I was able to bend over quite far and grab hold of my ankles. I continued praying that I would make it through this and be able to hold, hug, and see my children that night. I prayed that if I did not make it, God would watch over them and that they were raised right by their father, and live long, healthy, happy lives. I also prayed for and thought of all my family members and friends and was again relieved that they were not here with me and being spared this kind of terror. I prayed for all the "souls on board" the plane as well.

My prayers and thoughts were cut short as we heard Captain Haynes' command of "Brace, brace, brace!"

There were a few minutes of total silence and silent prayers. Then there was a sudden loud roar, and it felt like a punch to the stomach as the plane hit the ground and was being turned upside down, shaken up and thrown with such force that it would never stop. Our world and our lives were going to be that way also, never to be the same again. All in a split-second.

I was to later learn that the sudden, hard impact was so violent that it sent the plane up on its nose and into a cartwheel where it broke up into about five large sections and into thousands of pieces.

The only way I can describe it is to compare it to a fast, uncontrolled roller coaster ride in the dark. Except, on a real amusement park roller coaster ride, you know how long it will take and the outcome of it. My roller coaster ride was terrifying and unpredictable. Instead of fresh air blowing in your face, there was dirt, debris, and smoke all around us as we rode the tumbling, 290-ton metal beast. The main fuselage I was in travelled approximately one mile from the first point of impact before coming to rest upside down. The other four large pieces of the plane had been scattered all over, traveling wherever the force and speed took them. The nose of the plane, which was the cockpit, had snapped off like the tip of a pencil.

The plane was at its maximum weight that day, with 296 souls on board.

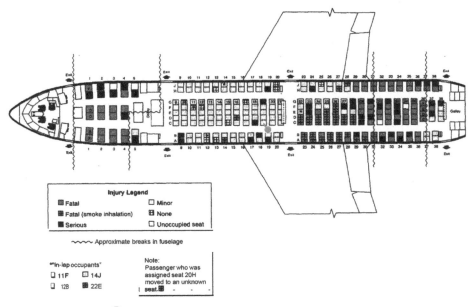

My seat, 19-C is in the main fuselage section that some of the survivors crawled out of.

3

THE CRASH

All of time seemed to stand still. I still replay the crash in my mind in slow motion because even though it took only minutes to totally destroy a fully loaded, large DC-10 airplane and to alter lives dramatically, it seemed like it was taking hours. The noise of the airplane being crushed and destroyed was so loud you could not hear yourself scream. I cannot remember screaming. I was too terrified to scream. The grinding and screeching of metal against asphalt, like fingernails scraping down a chalkboard in surround sound, was the only sound I noticed. It seemed as if I was in a different world or atmosphere. I had that same terrified feeling you get when your heart is in your throat and you are gasping for air, like a fish after it has been hooked and taken out of its element. Eyes wide open in terror and totally stunned into silence.

When the violent ride finally did stop, I realized I was still alive but very much in trouble. I did not know it at the time, but a large fireball exploded and rolled through the cabin as we were summersaulting. I was in the main fuselage that was the largest remaining part of the plane. It was also upside down. There would not be any mass exit sliding down the emergency slide that would have normally deployed from the plane. No. Those of us who could still function had to find a way out of the burning, broken, upside-down fuselage on our own. Being upside down and the plane being thrown in complete disorder during the crash down the runway had left me disoriented. Blood was rushing to my head, so I knew I was hanging upside down. My seat belt was the only thing holding me in place. I quickly unfastened it and fell on my head, hard. The fall was at least six feet, but it seemed much farther.

With so much debris lying around, plus the smoke and dirt that was settling, I could not see anyone else. I started calling Rod's name. He in turn was calling mine. Eventually, I saw his hand reach under some debris and grab mine.

"Are you all right?" was his first reaction.

"Yes, yes, I'm fine," I replied.

After moving some of the debris out of the way, he told me to follow him. Our seats were overturned above us. We were crawling on the ceiling of the plane! After crawling on our hands and knees to the right under the overturned seats, we were finally able to stand up. I later learned that some people who were still alive at that time perished in the roaring fire that eventually engulfed the fuselage. They had been unable to unfasten their seat belts. Part of the problem had to do with their weight, or they had been knocked unconscious or shocked into immobility.

After standing up, I was able to make a quick observation of my surroundings. Through one of the plane's windows, I saw the flickering orange-colored fiery glow of flames. Coughing from the thick smoke and dust that was engulfing the plane, I turned to follow Rod and a few other passengers toward an opening. It was only much later that I realized we had exited toward the front of the plane (where first class had been), not toward the rear as I had originally thought, and that this opening was eleven rows ahead of row 19 where I had been sitting. I later learned that the plane had broken in five different major pieces.

Rod suddenly stopped in front of me. He began helping some other men to extricate a woman that was trapped. The woman was later identified as Sister Mary Viannea. Debris pinned her into a small space with no way to get out. Her legs and hips had been badly bruised.

"Go on and follow the others," Rod told me.

"No, I'm fine. Get her out," I replied.

I halted so that they could help the woman. I did not realize that I should have kept moving as quickly as possible, since the whole fuselage was burning up around us. Within seconds, the men were able to get Sister Viannea free, and I followed them out of the nearest opening. Near the opening, I walked into some wire, got tangled up, and panicked a little bit. Rod helped me get untangled from the wire, then turned to me and told me to keep walking straight ahead, which led me into the cornfield.

I remember feeling like Dorothy in *The Wizard of Oz* as I stepped out of what used to be the ceiling and fuselage of the large DC-10. (The scene where her house lands, and she steps through the front door of her house into the land of Oz.)

"I'm going to change a lot of things that are wrong in my life," I said to myself. I could feel the imprint of the foot on my backside, which I knew belonged to God. He had just given me an alarming wake-up call to wake me up from the bad dream that was my current life.

The first thing I saw in front of me were cornstalks. Seven-foot-tall corn! There was corn in front of me and on all sides of me, with the burning fuselage behind me. Pure instinct and the reminder of Rod's words told me to follow all the others who were walking into the corn and away from the wreckage. Anything to put some distance from the fire, the smell of burning fuel and other smells that were associated with the now-furiously burning fuselage. Then there was a new smell. Something I had never experienced before and is now something that I will never forget. The smell of burning human flesh. Terrorized, with all my thoughts and movements on autopilot, I continued to try to find my way out of the corn.

As I was struggling to find my way out of the corn, with my soft pink high heels sinking into the soft soil, I did a quick assessment of myself. I was amazed to see that my clothes were not torn. Even though there was some blood on my skirt, I knew it was not mine. I did not even have a run in my hose! (I can run them just by looking at them sometimes.) I was going to have to praise Kim, my best friend from high school, who did my nails at the time, as I did not even have a broken nail.

Thus, the instinct, determination, and survival skills I was born with and implement into my everyday life kicked in. A little bit of blessed stubbornness always helps too. The saying "too stubborn to die" applies to me also. The total makeup of my being, my chemistry, my life, and my soul comes from a long, strong lineage of family history. When you think back on all the different veins of bloodlines that make up your family tree, it's amazing how you can be so much like one relative, close or distant, living or long ago dead, and yet still be your own unique self. It's when we must reach deep down inside ourselves that we realize what we are made of, and we are surprised by the strengths we have within us. How we hold onto that strength and what we do with it is entirely our own decision.

Physically, in build and facial features, I am very much like my mother. I am grateful and proud to look like her. She has beautiful bone structure and facial features that always light up her face and make you want to smile. Her inner beauty, combined with this gift she has for making you smile and want to enclose her in a warm hug, are only a couple of the features she is blessed with. While in the working world, she was always a smart dresser. Now, at the age of eighty-six, wearing overalls with stitching on them of Winnie the Pooh and other characters, women, young or old, will stop her to say hello and admire her overalls. She is a tiny person with a glow around her that attracts people to her while wearing those overalls. I'd like to think I have inherited and retained some of her better qualities. Although very petite, she is strong-willed, a trait that I have and that I have passed down to my daughter.

She was born in Fort Collins, Colorado, in 1935, the second child of three. A frail, tiny baby, she was carried around in a shoebox and was raised on goat milk, since she couldn't tolerate regular milk. The goat milk was the best thing for her, and she grew but was always very tiny and petite. Even though it saved her life and she prospered from it, to this day, she cannot drink any kind of milk. When she was five years old, her family moved to Log Cabin, Colorado, which is fifty miles north of Fort Collins. Her mother and father ran a small country store there in which her father was also the postmaster for the small community. Living in a remote rural area, in a small log house with only an outhouse and none of the amenities that we have today, she has happy memories of her first five years in Log Cabin. She started school and attended kindergarten through the fourth grade before her family moved to Indian Hills, Colorado. Indian Hills was another small, remote rural community then, and when my mother enrolled to start school, there was no fifth-grade class, so she was moved up to the sixth-grade class. Two years later, her family moved to Littleton, where she attended grades eight through twelve at Littleton High School, in which she graduated at age seventeen, in 1952.

Her senior year in high school was when she met my father. He was attending Petersburg School in Sheridan, Colorado. At the time, my mother's family was living in a small house near the school, and she would watch him from afar while he was at football practice. Her best friend Gloria was acquainted with him, and she told Gloria that she wanted to meet him. It happened on October 31, 1951 while at a Halloween dance at Petersburg school. Gloria introduced them, and they fell in love at first sight. Even though he was two grades behind her (due to his burn injury when he was twelve years old, he was set back one grade, and she had been advanced forward one grade), they were the same age—they were both born in February 1935.

For a year and a half after they first met, they dated steadily until there was a huge fallout. My mother wouldn't speak to him, and there was no other woman for him, so he decided to drop out of school and join the military after he turned eighteen. He turned eighteen in February of 1953 and joined the military in April. Come June, while he was still in basic training, he was informed that his father died of colon cancer. He was the only one at his father's funeral.

He never finished his eleventh and twelfth year of high school, and before he could join the paratroopers, he was required to have a high school diploma. He completed the requirements and earned a GED, which he was then able to submit to any high school that he had attended. Therefore, he submitted his GED to Middle Park

Union High in Granby, Colorado, which he attended prior to moving to Englewood where he met my mother. The school presented him with a genuine high school diploma. Afterwards, he was eligible to join and be a proud member of the 11th airborne division.

After several months of missing him and wondering where he was, my mother found him through the Red Cross. She wrote him a letter, enclosed a picture of herself, and the rest is history. The minute he received that letter and her beautiful picture, he called her and proposed over the phone. They were married shortly afterwards, on August 18, 1953. Both of them were just eighteen years old. They were married in the living room of the boarding house that my grandmother Hobson ran. It was a small wedding in which a few immediate family members attended to witness my beautiful mother in her lovely wedding dress marry my handsome father dressed in his military uniform. They were and still are the love of each other's lives.

My mother and father after twenty-nine years of marriage.

45

Chief Marion Hobson, 1982

My father is also extraordinarily strong willed. He possesses an aura of integrity and knowledge that overcomes any other weaknesses he may have. His strength comes from the hard knocks and lessons he learned while growing up in the Deep South during the Depression. He was born in Nashville, Tennessee, in 1935. Before he was born, his father became blind. The moonshine available in those early years of the 1930s was considered very harmful and poisonous. He learned that his father was a heavy whisky drinker and more than likely lost his sight due to the moonshine poison. His father never got to see his handsome son the whole time he was growing up. My father's nickname is Rip. He used to sleep more than normal when he was a baby; therefore, he was nicknamed after Rip Van Winkle, the story book character most of us know. Since his father was blind, his mother had become the breadwinner of the household. While she was at work, or searching for work, Rip became his fathers' eyes after he was old enough to help with things around the house, which in the late 1930s was the tender young age of five years old. He shared with me a couple of stories which he remembers vividly. One of them was when he was responsible for fixing his father's lunch. He would stand on a stool over the kitchen stove and boil hot dogs or heat up soup. For a young child, that was quite a feat. Another story was when he and his father had to beat a grass fire that was burning close to their home in rural Mississippi. He retrieved a rug for himself and his father, and they both tackled the fire as Rip shouted out to his father where the fire was popping up; left, right, behind, or in front. He proudly said that they were able to eventually put out the fire with neither of them getting burned.

After my Aunt Betty was born and a few years old, my grandfather was admitted to a convalescent home for the blind. He was not able to hold down a job; therefore, my grandmother had to leave him there and took my father and Betty with her. They had to move around from town to town, depending upon where my grandmother could find work for herself. My father, being almost ten years older than Betty, had to take responsibility for her when their mother was at work. Even at such a young age, he learned how to be responsible and to take care of others. He remembers having to move ten or twelve times to at least twelve different towns in a space of thirteen years, each time being awaken in the middle of the night, asked to gather his belongings and leaving wherever they were under the cover of darkness. His mother was eventually unable to pay the rent various times, so they kept moving around while she would try to find work. He recalls having to sleep in parks and bus stations. One time, while they were passing through Memphis, Tennessee, down on their luck, and sleeping in the bus station, a bus driver took them to his home for the night where they were fed and given a bed to sleep in. The next morning, the bus driver took them back to the bus station where they continued their journey. My father recalls that being the best night's sleep he had had in a long time during those lean years.

A few years later, when my father was twelve years old, while living in Pontotoc, Mississippi, both his legs were horribly burned. One day while he was at one of his friend's house, they discovered a can full of gasoline sitting outside on a bench. As curiosity got the better of them, and his friend being a prankster, lit a match and threw it into the can, causing a fire to flare up. In an attempt to put out the fire, his friend then swept the can off the bench. Unfortunately, it was swept toward where my father was standing. The gasoline fire splashed on my father's legs, and before he knew it, his jeans were on fire. He had been taught by his mother to roll on the ground in the dirt to put out a fire. Being very frightened, but still able to remember what his mother had taught him, he attempted to put the fire out by rolling in the dirt, all the while screaming very loudly. His screams were heard by the boy's mother who was inside the house. After sizing up the situation, she ran out to help my father. She grabbed him by his pant legs and lifted him upside down and shook him in order to get his jeans off. She burned both of her hands in the process which eventually healed, but my father ended up spending one year in the hospital. At first, the doctors wanted to amputate his legs since the burns were so severe, but my grandmother would not hear of it. He endured two skin grafts in which they took skin from his upper thighs and grafted the bottom half of his legs where they were burned. He was also immersed numerous times in a tub of water and iodine to keep any infection away. This is how he spent his sixth-grade year of school. Afterward, he had to learn how to walk again. He has always shown strength when up against adversity, and this incident put him to the test.

This strength and tenacity followed him throughout his life as he eventually worked his way through the ranks after joining the Littleton police department to later become chief. He attended Metropolitan State University of Denver and after four years of night school, he earned a master's degree in political science. While serving as chief he attended the FBI Academy in Quantico, Virginia, and finished second in his class, all the while helping my mother raise two teenage daughters.

I have never had any fear of flying. My first airplane flight was as a teenager when my mother, sister, and I flew to Virginia for my father's FBI graduation. At one point in his life my father also trained and received his pilot license and I recall being thrilled to fly with him.

Strength and Adversity:

- Adversity is like a strong wind. It tears away from us all but the things that cannot be torn, so that we see ourselves as we really are.

  —Arthur Golden

- Strength doesn't come from what you can do. It comes from overcoming the things you once thought you couldn't
- Fear is a reaction. Courage is a decision.
- One small crack does not mean you are broken, it means that you were put to the test and you didn't fall apart.

  —Linda Poindexter

After hearing these trials and triumphs and observing my father practically every day of my life, I realize where my strength comes from. It isn't from just one person. It comes from the chemistry, trust, and love that a family such as mine has.

"You are like a hitching post. You are so strong that people just want to hold onto you while they weather out the storms in their lives." This is how my father describes me.

I don't give up or give in easily. If I have a goal in mind that I need to reach, I simply set it and go after it. I complete what what I set out to do. The journey may be long and the work hard, but the reward for surviving long enough to reach your goal is something you can hold in your heart and mind and say, "I did it!" Whatever the goal is, it should be worth achieving and living for.

Two days after the crash, my father and I had lunch. It was the first time I had seen him since the crash, as he was out of town, and it took him longer than expected to get home. He had been on the road driving eighteen-wheelers. This was one of the things he had on his bucket list since he had retired as chief of police of Littleton. As I understood it, he was on the East Coast and could not get home as soon as he heard I had been in the crash. He had been in a hotel room waiting to finish his run when my mother called him with the news of the crash. The first thing she told him was that I was fine and had survived. When he turned on the television in the hotel room, he could not believe his eyes. It took a while for him to comprehend the magnitude of the visual he was seeing on the news. He got down on his knees then and there and said a long prayer in which he thanked the Lord for sparing me.

Our reunion and our lunch date was a very anticipated and special day for me. After sitting for hours over our lunch as I told him everything, he asked me, "What if you died on that plane? Where would your soul be now?"

Those two questions hit me right between my eyes. I had no idea where I would be if I perished. I only knew at the time that I was sitting across from my dear father and rejoicing that I could see him and talk to him as I always have when I had a major problem or needed him. He was and still is always there for me, my sister, and our mother.

Once I was out of the wreckage, I didn't know which way to go. I remember thinking about the others that were behind me and just getting as far away from the burning fuselage that I could without getting lost in the giant corn.

Not too far from the wreckage, I stumbled across a woman lying on the ground. Her leg was badly mangled, and she was in excruciating pain but coherent. Another fellow passenger was trying to help her and asked me for my belt to be used as a tourniquet. As I started taking off my belt, someone else appeared out of the corn and offered his. The two men used the belt to tourniquet the woman's leg, as a bone was protruding from her torn, bloody leg. I continued walking on through the corn, knowing there wasn't much else I could do. I wandered on as I could hear others around me trying to find their way out of the giant corn. Now I felt like I was in a dense, overgrown jungle. The heat of the July summer day, combined with the heat and smoke from the fire of the plane, plus the unsettled dust, made the air around me very suffocating. Eventually, after about ten minutes of stumbling through the corn, I came to the end of a row and was standing on a small hill in a clearing. All around me was corn, corn, and more corn; also, a stand of trees, a tower of some kind, and a dirt road. But what I also saw were more survivors! Who else but fellow passengers would be out in the middle of an Iowa cornfield on a lovely summer day?

While standing there trying to get acclimated to my surroundings, a distraught oriental woman came stumbling toward me. She didn't appear to be injured, just deeply distraught and out of her mind with grief. "I can't find my baby! Please help me find my baby! Have you seen my baby?" she cried out to me.

Before I could answer her, she turned, fell on her hands and knees, and crawled away. I felt as helpless as she did. I had no words of comfort to give her. Her name is Sylvia Tsao.

I later learned that her young son, Evan Tsao, aged two, had been ripped out of her arms upon impact. Children aged two and under could fly for free and placed on their mother's laps during flight. She had been holding him between her legs on the floor, in front of her seat as instructed before the crash. She had last seen him flying at a high rate of speed down the right aisle toward the back of the plane, headfirst as the plane was tumbling. He did not survive. His body was later found in the wreckage of the plane.

Jerry Schemmel tried to help Sylvia find Evan after he had exited the crashed plane. He had heard an infant crying somewhere in the wreckage and went back inside the burning fuselage thinking it was Evan. He pulled a baby out from an upside-down overhead bin, but it was not Evan. This was a baby girl.

I was still standing among the other survivors looking into the distance, which was about one-fourth mile away at the huge, black, billowing cloud of smoke that used to be the airplane. This was its final resting place, the crash site. As I was watching the cloud of smoke grow larger and larger, a man in a suit walked out of the corn right in front of me and handed me a baby.

"Could you please hold her? I don't know who she is or where her parents are."

"Sure," I said, taking the baby girl.

As he turned and left, I made some quick mental observations of the baby's condition. Being a mother myself, I could offer her as much comfort as I could, just by holding her and trying to reassure her. She was about one year old and dressed in a pretty summer dress. She wasn't crying or injured in any way that I could see. She had a small red welt on her cheek and had lost her diaper. Other than that, she appeared fine. I couldn't believe she wasn't even crying!

Not long after standing there, holding her and wondering what to do next, another man came running out of the corn straight at me. "Oh my God, my God!" he yelled. "You found my little girl!" He took her from my arms, as she was reaching out to him. She had recognized him as her daddy. "Thank you! Thank you!" he said to me.

I didn't get a chance to tell him that I had not been the one to rescue her, as he at once turned and approached a woman and two young boys who were emerging from the corn. Seeing them form a close-knit circle and embrace each other brought tears to my eyes. How I thanked God that my children were not on the plane with me! I later found out that Jerry Schemmel was the rescuer, and the family of five who all miraculously survived were the Michaelsons.

The baby girl's name is Sabrina Michaelson. She was traveling as one of the "lap" children, being held by her mother Lori when the plane hit the ground. Sabrina's father Mark was seated in the seat to the left of Lori and Sabrina. Sabrina's two older brothers were seated in the aisle behind their parents directly in back of them. The Michaelsons were leaving Denver to relocate to Cincinnati where Mark was to start a new job.

Sabrina slid out of her mother's grasp upon impact, traveling underneath the seats and out of sight. After Mark and his two sons were able to exit the wreckage, they saw Lori without baby Sabrina.

According to a journal staff writer for *the Sioux City Journal*, Mark asked Lori if she had the baby. Lori told him that she had lost her. Lori was quoted: "I frantically tried to hold my baby. She was screaming bloody murder. I was sobbing. 'Don't cry, Mom,' my son was saying as we crouched over in a crash position. Then there was a terrible jolt, the sound of crunching metal—the plane was flipping over. My baby was pulled out of my arms. I thought the floor had given way or that she had gone out a hole or a window. I didn't even have time to react, to try to tighten my grip. She was gone. My baby really didn't have a chance…it has to be a miracle." (*Reference Redbook Magazine,* November 1989, p. 130)

As Lori and her sons walked away from the burning fuselage, Mark immediately tried to go back inside the burning wreckage, all the while fighting against other evacuees as they were funneling out of the wreckage. He heard her crying, but could not see her. He had to turn away as the smoke and flames around him got worse. He set out to find his wife and two sons, checking with one group of survivors after another, to no avail. After frantically searching some more, he saw Sabrina in the arms of another survivor. Alive. Safe.

As mentioned, that woman was me, and the Michaelsons were soon reunited with each other. They all suffered abrasions and bruises in the crash, but nothing more serious or terrifying than losing their youngest member of the family.

When I read of her suicide, I could not believe it or wrap my head around it. Why had she done it? The only memory and picture I have of her is from that fateful day, July 19, 1989, as she was handed to me by a fellow survivor. Such a beautiful baby girl that had survived a major airline crash, with only a missing diaper and a bruise on her left cheek, to end up taking her own life only twenty days short of her twentieth birthday.

She has been described as a beautiful young woman who identified herself as the baby girl whose life was saved by a stranger (Jerry Schemmel). He had continuously, through the nineteen years since the crash, stayed connected with Sabrina and her family, receiving pictures and updates. After her death, he tried to find out more about what happened and the circumstances that led up to it but received no response from her family.

After searching the Internet for any information about Sabrina, I did find the picture that is on her cemetery plaque in the Queen of Heaven Cemetery in Mesa, Arizona, where she is buried. The plaque shows a couple of pictures of her at various ages, including one near the end of her life, with her Doberman. It is hard to associate this picture with the one that I will always carry in my mind of her on the day of the crash when she was placed in my arms by Jerry.

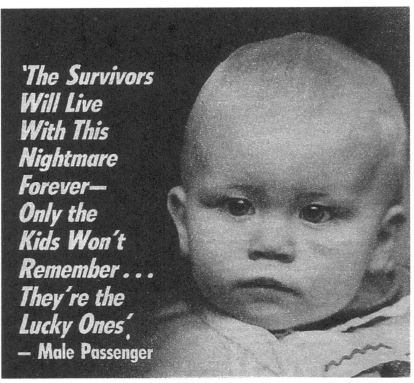

'The Survivors Will Live With This Nightmare Forever—Only the Kids Won't Remember . . . They're the Lucky Ones'
— Male Passenger

The above picture of baby Sabrina was taken shortly after the crash. The welt on her left cheek can be seen. Opposite page, the cemetery plaque at her final resting place.

I then turned my attention again to my whereabouts and decided I better follow the other survivors who were starting to walk along the dirt road. The road took us to a group of buses that responded when word was spread that there were survivors in the corn. The buses stopped abruptly when they saw the group of us walking toward them.

Before loading the bus, I saw one survivor gripping a Bible and silently praying. That scene left a significant impact on my memory. I realized that even though some of us had just survived what would be called one of the major airline disasters in the world, there was still a lot of surviving left to do. The sudden, abrupt, harsh change in our lives and the will to go on and get through it would be our greatest challenge and survival test yet to come.

These buses would eventually take us out of the cornfield and past the horrible, graphic scene of the path of destruction that the plane had left. Sitting in a seat on the bus by myself, I recall seeing destruction everywhere: pieces and parts, large and small from the airplane, luggage, clothes, seats, personal items, papers, books, magazines, wires, tires, metal, and white sheets lying in various places.

I was alive and able to function; however, suddenly, I realized that I had lost all my personal possessions. I had lost my purse, which had pictures of my children and money in the billfold. I also had no identity on me. No clothes. My purse, luggage, and the book I was reading were among the items that were left behind in the burning fuselage. After I processed this information, I realized that none of that mattered. I was going to be able to see my children, replace my identification, and buy new clothes that I would need. It was so much more than some of the other passengers were going to be able to do. I was grateful to be alive.

Although it wasn't an exceedingly long ride (no more than one mile) to the triage area, it seemed like a long way and took an eternity. The gruesome, violent aftermath that the bus had to pick its way through was enough to turn anyone's head away. However, instead of turning away, I couldn't help but stare. Human nature draws us to the bizarre and the unimaginable. If you've ever come upon a horrible car accident, you know what I mean. You stare all the while going by it until it's behind you. We seem to be drawn to things that are out of the ordinary, especially if we are on the outside looking in as if sitting in a movie theatre, watching an exciting or scary movie. We are there for the pure joy of anticipation, a relevant story, and the climax. We receive an adrenaline rush. We can handle this, as we know we can get up and walk away from it, leave it behind us. But this wasn't a movie set, and the people around me were not acting. This was real.

There was destruction, debris, people, and bodies everywhere. Various triage areas had already been set up. You could tell the difference between the crash victims and the rescuers, as the victims had a vacant, lost look in their eyes, and some were bleeding.

I saw a lot of white sheets lying randomly here and there, only to later learn and realize that these were the bodies of some of the passengers. Some of the bodies had yet to be covered and lay in the cornfield or on the runway in the hot July midday sun of Iowa. There was a low murmur of voices and soft crying from those of us on the bus as we passed the destruction and realized that any one of those bodies could have been one of us.

I was hoping that I was only dreaming and that I'd soon wake up.

The bus was slowly picking its way through the mayhem, which only prolonged the agony of having to see the aftermath and think of what could have happened to me.

I kept thinking, *That body lying there could be me.*

Feeling relieved one moment and guilty the next, it was hard to sort out exactly what my feelings were. Relieved that one of the bodies wasn't mine and feeling guilty that I was alive left me totally confused. What was I feeling? What were the other survivors feeling? A multitude of thoughts were coming and going through my head. My brain must have been on autopilot; I was in shock. How else could I have kept from breaking down and becoming hysterical?

After the bus stopped, a few of us were then asked to climb into the back of a truck bed. I can't remember what kind of truck it was, only that it had various tools and hoses in it and was smaller than a fire truck. From there, a handful of us were transported to a building. The building was the National Guard Armory that housed the Sioux City Iowa Air Guard, 185th Tactical Fighter Group. The Iowa National Guard happened to be meeting that day at the Sioux City base. This affected our rescue immensely, as there were numerous National Guard members present when the crash happened, and they were needed in a large way to help with the rescue. They couldn't have been in a better place at a better time.

Having previously been a member of the National Guard in Colorado, the building and its atmosphere was familiar to me. There was a sense of authority and order surrounding us. I found myself welcoming this authority, as I needed guidance after the disarray and confusion since the plane crashed.

Those of us who were upright, walking, and appeared to be physically uninjured were led to a large room that looked like a cafeteria. After sitting for a while in a shocked daze, my attention was drawn to a television that was mounted in one of the upper corners of the room. A sense of déjà vu came over me as I watched the scene on the television unfold. There was a massive airplane coming in for a landing, and as it tried to land, it crashed, flipping end over end!

Those of us watching it were spellbound and wondered why they were showing such a thing on television so soon after the plane we'd been flying in had crashed. Wasn't it enough to have to deal with what we'd just been through, we had to watch someone else's anguish also?

Only after we'd been watching for a couple of minutes did some of us realize, after reading the caption on the screen and listening to the announcer, that what we were seeing replayed over and over, was our airplane crash. A sense of disbelief and a feeling of denial was written all over everybody's face.

I heard someone say, "There's no way that could have been the plane we were in!"

The plane looked to be destroyed and in a million pieces. "How could anyone have walked away from that?" (We later learned that one of the hospital physicians arriving on the scene immediately afterward, while hovering over the crash site, stated he feared there were no survivors.) The crash scene looked like a war zone with equipment, destruction, smoke, fire, and bodies everywhere. We were all anxious to learn more about our fates as we kept watching the breaking news story. I was glued to the television, staring at it with my mouth open.

After a while, a man with some authority turned the television off and asked those of us surrounding it, "Please don't turn the television back on."

I found myself returning to the corner of the room that I had set my eyes on when first entering the building. After such a shock and horrible ordeal, I sought solitude, if only for just a few minutes. The enormous, overwhelming feeling made me want to curl up in a hole and wish the whole thing away. Perhaps I was just dreaming after drifting off to sleep, and I would wake up in my own bed and familiar surroundings. Only then would I sigh with relief that it was all just a dream, or a nightmare.

I saw a lot of compassion in the people around me. Whether they were other survivors or rescue personnel, they all had that concerned but kind, generous look on their faces. Everyone just wanted to comfort someone. Some faces were of desperation and fear also.

I remember thinking to myself that I was going to be looking at things differently, that I was going to try to avoid the negativity and rudeness in people and try to look for the good. I was determined to change a few things in my life.

Sitting on the floor with my knees drawn up and my arms clasped around them, and my head down, I looked up when a kind, gentle voice asked, "Are you all right?"

I replied, "Yes, I think so. Actually, no. No, I'm not. Physically, I think I'm all right. I really don't know." Obviously, I was in shock and confused.

I was looking into the handsome face of a fellow passenger I remembered seeing earlier that morning in the terminal and at the boarding gate. I had walked behind him while boarding the plane in Denver. I specifically remember him since he was quite tall, young, and good-looking.

"I don't think any of us are all right, are we?" I asked.

4

I Am Alive

As is proper when two strangers meet, we introduced ourselves. His name was Garry Priest, and he also was traveling on a business trip with his boss Bruce Benham. Bruce also survived and walked away from the crash. Although we really didn't know what to say, we eventually found some comforting words for each other. Garry seemed unharmed, except for a black eye and a small red spot on his eye which could have come from anywhere. He may have bumped it during impact or scratched it on a cornstalk. I didn't inquire about it since it didn't seem to be a concern to him. He was more concerned about me. I was fine physically, as far as I knew. I had not broken a nail, run my hose, or torn my clothes. I'm sure I smelled like dirt and smoke, though. However, mentally and emotionally, I wasn't sure how strong I was at that time.

We established and formed a bond at once. A lot of friendships and bonding for life took place that day. It's amazing how in one instant you are complete strangers, and the next instant, you are bonded for life due to a life-changing, split-second event. Your body chemistry and outlook on life are forever altered. The things you once thought important aren't so important anymore. The situations that you find yourself stressed out about don't seem that important when you realize your life could have been snatched away and quickly ended, or forever changed physically as well as mentally.

Not too long afterward, we were told that there were a couple of telephones available for us to use to call family, friends, or anyone we needed to contact about our well-being. Most of us began forming a line to wait our turn to make that important phone call. After waiting awhile, it was finally my turn. Being in the state of mind I was in, it was difficult for me to remember the phone numbers of my parents, sister, and in-laws. Deciding on who to contact first was a difficult decision. I wanted to be able to talk to everyone I loved at once.

After remembering her phone number and knowing that my sister was home with her five-month-old son, I decided to call her first. I so very much needed to talk to someone who was close to me so that I could draw some comfort just from hearing their voice. As the phone rang, I prayed that she was home and was able to answer. As soon as I heard her voice, I was overwhelmed with relief and emotion.

"Babette, it's me, and I'm all right!"

"What do you mean? What happened, where are you?" she asked, hearing the strain and emotion in my voice.

"Have you been watching television?" I asked. "Our plane crashed. I'm in Iowa. I'm sure it's all over the news by now. Don't worry though, I'm fine. I walked off without a scratch," I replied.

She told me that she was not aware of the crash as she was watching a movie channel.

"Turn on the local news station. I'm sure it will show coverage of the plane crash and everything that is going on now," I encouraged her.

After doing so and uttering her disbelief that I was okay, I asked her to call my in-laws and assure them that I was fine. I knew my mother-in-law was home and that my kids, Bryson and Molly, would be at her house after their day at Lakeside with their dad. I also asked her to call our mother and father at work and tell them that I would try to call them later. There were still some people waiting to contact loved ones, and I didn't want to tie up the phone for too long.

"Are you sure you're all right?" she asked.

"Yes, I'm fine. There are a lot of people here helping us. I love you. I'll see you soon. I'll call you again when I have a chance."

As I hung up the phone, I realized just how fortunate I was to be able to physically pick up the phone and talk to a loved one. It was a miracle that I was sitting there, physically unharmed, and alive! I felt reassured that Babette would contact everyone for me and put their fears at ease when they realized that I had been in a major plane crash that was making headline news across the country, and that I had survived.

Taking one thing at a time, my next step was to sit and wait until those of us who were uninjured could be transported to the hospital for observation and a checkup.

Riding in the back of an ambulance while you are alert and unharmed is by far the more acceptable situation. Sitting up and talking to other passengers, I could almost believe I was riding as just another passenger in a family vehicle on the way to a certain destination, except for the wail of the siren and the unfamiliar faces and scenery surrounding me. I was still in shock and quite numb to the various conversations taking place among those of us riding in the back of the ambulance on the way to the hospital.

However, I caught phrases such as "I can't believe this has happened!" or "What seat and aisle were you sitting in on the plane?" "What did you see?" or "How do you feel?" These questions were being tossed back and forth like a game of hot potato. Nobody wanted to give an answer, but we all had many questions. We were all caught up in our own horror, grief, and numbness; there were not any good, positive answers to respond with. We realized all at once that our lives had just been forever altered. The situation was very disturbing and scary to think about.

For some of us, it was the solution to an unhappy marriage, or the solution to repairing some other problem in our lives that up until now was irreparable. It's amazing how many solutions or situations you can act out in your head after you've been given the strength to finally approach them and deal with them. Suddenly, you may feel invincible! You just survived and walked away from a major plane crash. You are capable of anything now, except for comprehending what just happened and how it could have happened to you!

The ride to the hospital was not an exceptionally long one, which I was grateful for. I was feeling very vulnerable and getting irritated with one woman's repetitive questions and statements. There are times when you just want to shut out all the noise that is assaulting your ears.

5

THE HOSPITAL

Upon arriving at Marian Hospital (Marion is my father's first name; the thought gave me some comfort and encouragement), a throng of doctors and nurses greeted us, eager to help us and give us a thorough checkup. I wondered why there were so many of them there all at once and later learned that the plane crash happened just when the shift change between the morning and evening shifts was occurring for both hospitals. This doubled the staff on duty at the hospitals, and all the staff in both hospitals had been asked to stay due to the major catastrophe that just happened in their hometown.

The expressions of compassion and sorrow on the faces of the nurses and doctors told me that those of us who just arrived in our ambulance were among the fortunate ones. Even though we were able to walk, we were wheeled through the hospital doors in wheelchairs. The doctors and nurses that were waiting for yet another arrival of an ambulance full of plane crash victims went to work at once as the ambulance arrived.

There was a commotion and a flurry of activity all around me. Since the more seriously injured victims had already arrived, the minorly injured patients had been lined up against the hospital hallways, waiting their turn for a medical evaluation. I was among the people who were asked to wait patiently.

Numerous nurses who walked by told me, "Someone will be along shortly to gather information and assist you." Knowing that they had so many other seriously injured patients to attend to and that I had nowhere else to go, I settled in to wait.

Still being in shock, I saw the activity going on around me as one would while dreaming. A lot of things still did not make sense and seemed out of proportion. There were people in white, blue, and green medical coats hurrying from one end of the hallway to another; going in and out of rooms. There were many gurneys crammed together along the wall of the hallway I was in. On some of the gurneys, there were dazed and confused patients like me. Others held injured and bleeding patients, but even though they were injured, they were coherent. I could see the injured moving their heads and looking around from time to time. As I lay there, the scenario of the crash kept playing itself over and over in my mind. I had lost all track of time. I did not know if it was still afternoon, early or late evening. I was not hungry, hysterical, or crying. I just wanted to be examined and on my way. I needed some closure to the day but did not realize that would not happen for quite a while.

Finally, I was taken into an X-ray room and examined. The exam itself did not take long. A couple of X-rays, a blood pressure and heart rate check, some poking and prodding were all that were necessary to verify that I did not have any life-threatening physical injuries.

My neck was sore, my eyes burned like I was still inside the burning plane, but other than that, I was diagnosed as being "fine." I could not wait to take the contacts out of my eyes. It was like being under water with my eyes open. Everything was blurry, and it hurt to keep them open. However, I would not have been able to see very well, if at all, without them. As uncomfortable as they were, I did not want to relinquish them for fear I would not be able to see at all. I needed some form of vision to make sure that things were real and not just a dream that I was looking from the outside into.

The next thing I remember is being ushered back into an ambulance and taken away from the hospital. I had no idea where we were being taken. I don't even remember any other passengers in the ambulance. All at once, we arrived at what looked like a dorm on a college campus. It looked dreary in the waning sunlight, so I determined it was at least the early hours of the evening. Time did not stop at all that day; it passed slowly. Evening was coming, and I welcomed the end of this fateful, traumatic day. I did not know it at the time, but that night would be the longest one I have ever had.

Briar Cliff College, now known as Briar Cliff University, is situated on a scenic hilltop on the outskirts of Sioux City, just minutes from downtown. There are four residence halls. I do not remember which one I stayed in, I just know that it was a temporary haven for some of us passengers who needed a quiet place, away from all the carnage and mayhem that had surrounded us earlier that day. However, not all the survivors were staying at the college dorm. Some others had been brave enough to fly home that evening. Others were able to stay in a generous Sioux City resident's home that was offered.

After being guided into the dorm, I was given a room with two beds in it. They were your average college dorm beds, but under the circumstances, they looked extremely comfortable and inviting. My roommate's name was Ruth Pearlstein. (Ruth is my mother's first name. I could only think that this was a positive omen.) Ruth and I introduced ourselves and fell into a quiet, easy conversation. I can't recall the exact words that were exchanged, but I do remember that she was engaged to be married very soon.

After a while, I realized that I felt very gritty and dirty. All I wanted to do was take a shower and crawl into bed and pull the covers over my head. Just maybe I could make the entire day disappear if I tried to push it away and forget it. I had no toiletries to shower with or clothes to change into. However, I was told that the Red Cross had brought some clothes, shoes, and toiletries for us to have. The articles were all laid out on long tables in another room in the dorm. By the time I was able to "shop" for what I needed, everything had been well-picked over. I ended up with a much too large pair of pink sweats, exceptionally large underwear, and tennis shoes that were about one size too big for me. The toiletries were not what I was used to, but then again, I was not in a frame of mind to really care and was just grateful for what I was provided. I had never received this kind of courteous attention before and felt very comforted by the Red Cross volunteers by the time I went to take my shower.

I was alone in the girls' dorm bathroom. It was a relief to finally be alone for a while. It was even more of a relief to get out of my clothes that had been permeated with the smell of smoke, dirt, sweat, and the burning airplane, and all it had consumed.

As I was taking my shower, a flood of grief that was stronger and hotter than the water in the shower overcame me. It came pouring out of me as if a dam had broken. I sobbed and cried in the shower stall until my eyes were tired and my head was swimming and aching. I had hoped that the sound of the running water would drown out my grieving sounds. I didn't know which emotion to feel first: the relief that I was alive, the guilt of being alive while others had perished, the loneliness of being in a strange place without any familiar faces around, or the sadness of the whole ordeal. Flashes of the scenes I had seen also came to the front of my mind and memory. I wished that they all could have just washed down the drain with my tears, never to return. However, I had to gather myself together, get dressed, and face the night and whatever it would bring.

I found out all too soon that the night would be long and sleepless, with a never-ending image of flashbacks playing themselves out over and over in my mind. I was exhausted, yet sleep would not come. I was too wound up, with too much time on my hands, and nothing to do with it. Concentration on anything other than the crash was out of the question also, as there was so much to think about and so many questions to ask and have answered. There was an abundance of food laid out on various tables available for those of us in the dorm, but I had no appetite.

I couldn't call my children, as I was sure they would be asleep. Knowing that Mommy was going to be gone for the night anyway and being too young to understand what I had just been through, I was sure that they were comfortable and snug, asleep in their beds at home.

Insomnia and confusion are what sent me wandering the halls of the dorm through the night. While talking to others and listening to their grief and description of our trauma, and watching the endless new reports on television, the night finally unfolded. There were a lot of different news stories, coverage of the crash and surviving passengers' stories as they were interviewed. I watched a lot of them for quite a while, still shaking my head in disbelief. This could not be happening. It had to be a dream.

Near dawn, I went back to my room, took off the large, hot sweats and was able to lie down and close my eyes. I was exhausted, however, that peace only lasted about one hour. I jerked awake out of a sound but short sleep. I was still in Sioux City, Iowa, in a college dorm room, not in a pleasant hotel room in Chicago where I was supposed to be. The realization of the previous day and my situation washed over me and hit me hard. I knew I could not just lie there and pretend it did not happen. I had to find my way home. I washed my face and put back on the too-large pink clothes and shoes that the Red Cross had given me and wondered how I was to get home.

6

WHAT TO DO?

One of the hardest things for me to understand the morning after the crash was that even though people were kind to us survivors, they were also oblivious to our feelings of wanting to get home the most comfortable way we needed. It didn't have to be the fastest, but some of us, including me, were not ready to get back on another airplane just yet. It was too soon.

After inquiring about car rentals, we found out that all the press and United personnel had rented all the cars that were available in the area. For some reason, the bus was not a possibility either. I was not in a situation where I could call home and ask someone to drive 650 miles (a ten-hour drive) from Littleton, Colorado to get me. So I was left with the only other choice available: another plane ride. It took me awhile to decide if this is what I really wanted to do. I kept changing my mind and going back and forth with my decision. It came down to one of the United personnel being rude to me regarding my indecision that I finally made up my mind. Various flights were coming and going back to Denver. I needed to be on one of them.

In my opinion, the transportation of us survivors to our home or final destination was not handled very well. I suddenly felt like I had done something wrong, instead of being the victim. How could anyone think that we would be willing and able to get back on an airplane after what we had just been through? Speaking for myself, I didn't think that I could do it! I weighed the options, and even though none of them appealed to me, my desire was to be able to get home to my children as quickly as possible. That thought outweighed anything else. Finally, I was booked on a flight to Denver. I thought it was a direct flight.

Those of us who were going to fly home were drove to the airport. While waiting in the small airport for the flight that would take me home, I witnessed a lot of activity that was going on around me. I saw that Ruth, my roommate from the previous night, had her fiancée by her side for encouragement and support. How I wished a loved one of mine was there with me to lean on and reassure me! Tears that started then did not let up until much later.

There was a lot of security control in the gate area where I waited. It was as much to keep the press out for us to maintain our privacy as for anything else. I remember needing to use the restroom and asking a security guard where they were. He looked at me as If I were some transient, instead of the crash victim that I was. I was sure that with the clothes I had on and carrying a paper bag that had the clothes I had worn on the plane in it, I did not look like a "normal" passenger.

"It's over there." He pointed in a general direction. "If you leave the secured area, you'll have to reenter through security again," he said.

My grief and frustration were rising to the surface of my emotions. "I am one of the survivors of yesterday's crash. I only have the clothes on my back. I only want to get home. Do I look like someone who is a threat?" I replied.

His expression softened. "When you come back, let me know so that I can waive you through."

I thanked him and went in search of the restroom. As promised, the guard waived me through the gate which was a large act of kindness considering the state I was in. After a couple of hours of anxious waiting, with only my paper bag full of my smoke-infested clothes and shoes to carry on, I boarded another plane. I had been given some medication, if needed, to help me stay calm as I started my journey home. Realizing that I was still in a state of shock also explained the numbness in which I boarded the plane. However, much to my disbelief, I learned that it was not a direct flight; we had to make a stop in Lincoln, Nebraska. We had to land and take off twice!

Instead of talking and interacting with the other passengers (some of them were survivors like me), I kept to myself, found my seat which was next to a window, and buried my head in my arms. I was hoping the medication would take effect very soon, as I remembered that my last thought when I was exiting the burning fuselage was that I felt like Dorothy in *the Wizard of Oz*. How I wished I could become her, tap my heels together and be home! The tears that had started earlier that afternoon came and went. I felt like I was the only one on this journey, with no interaction with anyone. I knew that my family was going to meet me in Denver, but I wanted someone right there and then to hold my hand and comfort me. Even after taking the medication to calm me, I was terrified when the plane lifted off the ground. Visions of it crashing to the ground and cartwheeling flashed through my mind. I kept my face buried in my arms and sobbed quietly.

7

HOME

During the flight to Lincoln, Nebraska, all I could think about was how are they going to land this plane safely? I didn't have any confidence in anything anymore. I stayed put in my seat—no one approached me or spoke to me. Even the airline attendants left me alone. My body language told them all they needed to know. My stress level was sky-high, and all I could do was pray for a safe landing, which we did have. I am thankful I didn't have to change planes then, as I would have chosen to walk to Denver instead of getting on another airplane.

Only when we had safely landed in Lincoln did I raise my head to reassure myself that we were on the ground and that I was still sitting safely in my seat, not hanging upside down after a vicious roller coaster ride through a cornfield. Suddenly, a rude voice interrupted my thoughts. "You are in my daughter's seat. She is boarding the plane here in Lincoln." The man that I was oblivious to, that was sitting next to me, was talking to me.

"Just what do you want me to do about that?" I replied.

My tone of voice must have made him realize I was in no mood to be reckoned with or told what to do. My tear-stained face should have told him even more. But from the way he acted, I don't think that he even acknowledged my situation or realized that I was one of the crash victims.

As he got up to find another seat, I heard him mumble, "They put all of the people from that plane crash on this plane. Now my daughter doesn't have a seat." He left my side in search of his daughter.

I was shocked by his behavior and wanted to tell him he was lucky she was able to get on this plane, that at least she wasn't one of the unfortunate ones lying on the runway back in Sioux City. (I had learned that the National Guard had to leave the dead victims where they came to rest after the plane crashed and broke apart on the runway and in the cornfield overnight.)

This man was just the first of many rude, uncaring people I was to later encounter.

As we took off from Lincoln, headed for Denver, I stayed in my current state of shock and numbness. I wanted to be left entirely alone while I thought of reuniting with my family when we landed in Denver. I hoped these thoughts could keep my mind from straying to the fact that I was yet again traveling thirty-seven thousand feet in the air in a large metal, mechanical airplane, where anything could go wrong.

I did a lot of praying the closer we got to Denver and another landing. When the wheels touched down and bounced on the runway, my heart jumped into my throat, and I gasped. I cringed, wringing my hands, until we came to a final stop at the gate.

While we were waiting at the gate to disembark the plane, we were informed that those of us who were on Flight 232 had the opportunity to meet with our family members in a private room in the terminal. We were also told that the press was waiting just inside the terminal doors and that there would be a lot of reporters, lights, and interaction. (These were the days when people were allowed in the gate terminal to say goodbye or wait to greet passengers just arriving.) Carrying my brown paper bag with my dirty smoke-filled clothes and shoes I had worn on the plane just the day before, somehow, I was able to avoid the press and was escorted at once to a specific room where my family was. As I stepped through the doorway, the first, most wonderful thing I saw were my two children. To be able to see them, hold them, hug, and kiss them was something I knew I would never get tired of or take for granted the rest of my life.

My seven-year-old daughter Molly asked me, "Mom, how did you survive that crash?"

"God saved me so that I could come home to you," I told her.

As young as they both were, I don't think they could grasp the multitude of what I had just been through. Both Bryson and Molly returned to being my "normal" children soon after I returned home.

I could not believe it had been only twenty-four hours ago that I was walking out of a burning fuselage into a cornfield. Now as I looked around the room, I saw my mother, mother in-law, father in-law, and my husband. I remember hugging the rest of my family and not wanting to let them go. My father was out of town and not expected until the next day, and my sister was at home with her infant son. Thankfully, I did get to see my father and sister within the next couple of days.

Soon after returning home, the phone started ringing off the hook. I was reluctant to answer it, as I was not ready to talk to anyone about my ordeal. We did not have an answering machine, and this was before cell phones, so I did not know who those first callers were. However, later in the afternoon, I did answer a call. They identified themselves as Harpo Productions and wanted to interview me and a few of the other survivors on the *Oprah Show* the following day. Knowing that the *Oprah* show taped in Chicago, I knew I was not going to be able to do it.

"I am not getting on another airplane tomorrow. I just got home, and I am not in any state of mind to travel so soon," I replied.

The caller was very apologetic and said that I would not have to travel to Chicago. They would tape me from a studio in Denver. They would provide transportation for me, and I would be able to watch the show that same afternoon from home. We made the necessary arrangements and designated time for the next day. After I hung up, I was in such a state of mind that I wasn't convinced that the phone call was official. However, if it was, I thought I should be prepared and was concerned about what I was going to wear and that I had no makeup. I lost everything on the plane. I decided that a quick trip to the store was in order.

Later that evening, once I was able to settle my kids down and put them to bed, and since I had no luggage to unpack, I hoped I would be able to get some rest if I could shut my mind down. If I was to be up early the next morning to be ready for a car to pick me up to take me to a studio in Denver to be on the *Oprah Show*, I needed to be prepared. A good night sleep will usually help the problem or situation appear minimal the next day.

Try as I might, I could not shut my brain off. It kept replaying the scenes and situations from the last twenty-four hours of my life. As exhausted as I was from lack of sleep the night before, I could not get to sleep. I wandered back and forth between my children's rooms, just looking at them peacefully sleeping and being thankful that neither of them had been on that plane and had not been a victim of the crash. They would be able to learn enough about it as they grew older. Right now, I just wanted them to stay the sweet, innocent children that they were. I wanted to be the parent to raise them, not their father or someone else. I thanked God and said many prayers that night before I was finally able to close my eyes for a couple of hours of sleep.

8

THE OPRAH WINFREY SHOW

July 21, 1989
My interview and other survivors

When I awoke the next morning, I was still on autopilot. I went through the motions of my morning routine and those of the kids. Knowing that I was going to be filmed for television, I put on an unusual amount of makeup. (Later when I watched the show, I could not believe how much makeup I had on!) At the due time, a limousine arrived to take me downtown Denver to the "studio." I was surprised by the limo, thinking that it was just going to be a taxi driver or something similar. I felt incredibly special being a passenger in a limo. However, once we arrived at the "studio," I was hesitant. It was just a small room, with the camera, the camera operator, and me.

The camera operator had me sit in a special spot, pinned a microphone to my shirt, put an earpiece in my ear, adjusted the lights, tested the sound, and instructed me to listen for Oprah's cue to me. It was all very professional but still seemed a bit impersonal. I did as he instructed, and soon I heard Oprah's introduction of the show and her guests.

The following is the transcript of the show that I later received on VCR tape from Harpo Productions.

Oprah said, "Once again you're watching the horrifying crash landing of DC-10 Flight 232. A scene from one of our worst nightmares. A terrifying picture of death, and while the word tragedy pales with the actual emotional aftermath of loss amidst the debris, sprang the jarring miracle of human survival. Today we are devoting this hour to the memory of the souls that perished, to the loved ones we hold in our prayers who are still trying to survive and to those who started down the barrel of death at exactly 4:04 p.m. two days ago and survived. One of the most incredible stories of survival comes from the Michaelson family who join us live by satellite from Sioux City, the town of that disaster. Imagine the horror of parents Lori and Mark to escape the blazing inferno with two of their children and discover that their baby girl (you see her holding right now) was still missing. And though Mark returned to the smoke-filled plane to find her, thirty gut wrenching minutes passed before they found that their one year old daughter had been rescued by an unknown hero and placed safely in the arms of another survivor; this woman, Margo Crain who joins us now by satellite from Denver, Colorado. Despite her joy for the Michaelson's Margo calls the whole experience horrifying, says she will never forget the screams of terror from passengers; sounds she believed were the last she would ever hear."

While introducing the Michaelsons and me, the camera showed the Michaelsons, Lori, and Mark with two of their children. Mark was holding his young son on his lap, and Lori was holding baby Sabrina on her lap. Both children, of course, were oblivious to the moment, and each were squirming in their parents' laps. Sabrina had a pacifier in her mouth, and their son was caught on camera yawning. Oh, the innocence of children. I was shown patiently listening with my earpiece, but with an expression of nervousness on my face. When Oprah said my name, I gave a small smile and shook my head, still in disbelief. Whether it was disbelief that I had survived the crash or that I was on the *Oprah* show, I'm not sure. I was still in a period of shock, and the moment seemed very surreal.

Oprah proceeded to interview the three guests that were live at the studio in Chicago: Ron May, Debbie Bellevue, and Tom Engler. (Afterward, when I was home later that afternoon, I watched myself on the *Oprah Show*. I recalled Debbie Bellevue as the woman I rode in the ambulance with from the crash site to the hospital. She was very animated and outspoken during that ride, and all I could think of was that I wished she would keep her thoughts and opinions to herself! Years later, I saw Tom Engler at both the twenty-fifth and thirtieth year anniversaries. Only then did I remember him being one of the guests on *Oprah*.)

Throughout the show, they had been trying to get audio from Sioux City where the Michaelsons were. After about twenty minutes into the show, there was still no audio with Sioux City, so Oprah began to interview me. There was no one to look at other than the camera, so I looked down a lot while trying to gather my memories.

She asked me if I could hear her. I replied yes. She then told me that they were having trouble hearing the Michaelsons and went ahead to ask me my account of the crash, where I was sitting, what I felt and saw.

"I was in row 19, seat C. I had to crawl toward the other side of the plane just to get out. When I did get out, it was just an eerie feeling because you were in the middle of a cornfield, and you expected to be on the runway. The man I was sitting next to was an ex-Navy pilot, and he was pretty reassuring through the thing, and he helped pull me out, and when we got out of the plane, he told me to just walk. Walk through the field and get away from here. So I did. And I ended up by a clump of trees, and this man, he gave me little Sabrina. He said, 'Here, could you please hold her? I don't know who she belongs to.'"

Oprah then asked me if this man was the Navy pilot. I said, "No, this was another man. I don't who he was."

Oprah then said, "He just came up to you and said take the baby?" I replied, "Yes. I think he was going to go back and help, so I just took her. She wasn't crying, she was so calm. She was just quiet. She had a small welt on her left cheek and had lost her diaper, but I just stood there holding her for a few minutes, reassuring her, and then her dad came running up and grabbed her and me and said, 'God, thank you, thank you!' That's the last I saw of them. I just started wandering off in another direction toward some other survivors to see if I could help anybody."

Oprah said, "So you just walked off into the cornfield. Were other people just walking in the cornfield, I guess trying to understand or comprehend what had happened?"

"Yes. You really didn't know which direction to go. The corn was really high. Some others around me said to just keep walking this way. I saw one woman lying in the cornfield, her leg was badly broken and mangled. It was the worst I saw at that time. I didn't see anything or anyone on the runway, or anything like that. Then an oriental lady came up to me and just fell at my feet. She said, 'I saw my little boy fly out of the plane. I don't know if he's dead or alive!' You are just standing there in awe or shock. You don't know what to do or where to go. I saw the smoke. The corn was hiding most of the plane wreckage. All I could see was a bunch of smoke."

Oprah said, "Yes, it's interesting that you mention Margo, the shock, because I wonder as this is happening; the plane is flipping over, and it happens so quickly. The mind. Your eyes see it, but the mind doesn't even have a chance to even comprehend it since you've never experienced anything like this before. When does the shock really set in?"

"It probably really set in that night when I was able to be by myself, with nobody around. I was taking a shower. I was standing in the shower, and it hit me then. It came and went. I'm up and I'm down. It comes and goes."

Oprah said, "In terms of crying or depression, or what."

"Yes, the crying and…"

Oprah said, "Yes, I can imagine. Let me ask you this Margo because it's a question I've been asking just reading about all of you who have experienced this miracle in your lives. Why do you think you survived?"

"I don't know. You know, you say why them, why me. Why did they die. Why didn't I. I just followed the procedures that I was instructed by the attendants and I just stayed in my position as long as I could. And then when we did stop turning and sliding and whatever we were doing I did let go of my seat belt. And then I fell on my head and was crumpled in a ball and I couldn't move. Then some stuff fell on me. Then Rod Vetter who I was sitting next to did pull me out. He then said come this way. People were relatively calm and helping those who couldn't get out, get out. Two men were carrying a sister off that was trapped and they pulled her out. I told them to get her out. That I was fine, I could walk. But what was really eerie was when I looked up and saw a cracked window and a fiery glow. That was really eerie and, I thought, oh my gosh, it's going to explode. I said, "we've got to get out of here." But there wasn't too far to go before we were out of the plane because the entire back of the plane was gone."

Oprah said, "I have since wondered since this is what the entire country has been talking about, it's been on all of our minds since it happened, how you then get up and go to work the next day. Have you been carrying on "quote" as normal or trying to?"

"Trying to. I was very afraid to fly home yesterday, and I debated between driving back and flying. But I was encouraged by my mother. She said, "you've got to do it sometime." And I said, "you're right." I do go to Chicago two, three times a year on business. I was going on business. I had to do it. I wanted a non-stop flight, but I didn't get one. From Sioux City to Lincoln was the hardest. The taking off and the landing was the worst part."

Oprah said, "You did it by yourself?"

"Yes. The second part of the trip from Lincoln to Denver was a little bit easier, but the first part of the trip back to Denver was really tough."

Oprah said, "It was mentioned earlier about your mind fully comprehending it. I still think that you all seem so normal to me. My guests here live today and your ability to talk about it. Do you think it all has really sunk in?"

"I don't think so. There was a mental health personnel at the shelter. He said, 'You all are handling it too normal right now. It will sink in. You will be up and down. You'll go back and forth. You will need to talk about it. Don't hold it in, talk about it.'"

Oprah said, "Have you all been talking about it? Other than to me. To family members, you've been able to talk about it?"

One of the guests said, "Sure, plus every newspaper in North America." (Chuckle from Oprah and the audience.) "The news media has been really good though. Real professional people."

Oprah was finally able to get audio from the Michaelsons, who were in Sioux City, via satellite. They had video as well as audio now. The camera showed Mark and Lori Michaelson, with baby Sabrina sitting on Mark's lap. All were smiling. In the background, you can hear baby Sabrina as Oprah asked Lori about her feelings of surviving the crash, only to discover that she had lost her baby. She mentioned that she had just talked to me, who had her baby after the crash, and asked Lori how she lost her. Lori explained how the flight attendant told her to put Sabrina on the floor so she could get into the crash position, and how uncomfortable she was about doing that. Lori wanted to hold Sabrina on her lap so she could keep a good grip on her. Lori put Sabrina on the floor. She said that things were very confusing. She was trying to cushion Sabrina with pillows as Sabrina was struggling to get off the floor, all the while she was also trying to keep her six-year-old son's head down. She was afraid that we would impact, and she wouldn't have hold of her.

Oprah asked her if Sabrina was between her feet. Lori said that she was and that she was trying to hold her stable with her legs. However, when the plane impacted, Sabrina "got sucked out of my hands." Her husband Mark was sitting behind her with their four-year-old son. Their six-year-old son was telling his mom (Lori) not to cry. Lori said that she didn't think that her two sons really knew what was going on. Oprah then asked Mark how he was handling all of it. He said he was obviously concerned about Lori and the baby and his son in front of them, but that his son sitting next to him was calm. He told his son that it was going to be rough, like an amusement park ride. They practiced the brace position.

After the explosion occurred, Mark must have changed seats with one of his sons. According to the passenger list both of his sons were listed as seated in row 12, seats D and E, behind Mark, Lori and Sabrina who were in row 11.

Oprah mentioned that she had earlier asked me about the fact that some people and family members did not make it, and what the Michaelsons thought the reason their entire family survived was. Mark said that he had no answers. When he came out of the corn and saw me holding Sabrina, he rejoiced. But then he saw another woman, and she asked him how he found his baby. (This must have been Sylvia Tsao, who was looking for her baby Evan.) Mark said that even as he felt rejoiced and happy at finding Sabrina, he felt the tragedy of this poor woman who was also a parent. Mark and Lori felt that one of their children was destined for greatness. "We're not sure which one, maybe Sabrina."

After I listened to and watched this interview and heard this statement by Mark, it saddened me to know that Sabrina did not live long enough to become destined for greatness. Knowing this as I write and collect my thoughts and see Sabrina as she was then is very disheartening. We all travel certain paths in our lives and make certain decisions from our choices, all of which get us to where we are, this day, this minute. Some of us are fortunate enough to be able to endure and figure it out; others are not so fortunate.

Oprah asked Mark if he thought that even though she's sure everyone followed instructions (as I had stated), if he thought that the proximity of where they were sitting on the plane had some effect on why they all survived. They had been sitting in rows 11 and 12.

Mark said that it seemed a very orderly evacuation from our section even though there were some people who were bleeding and seemed injured.

Oprah asked if we were afraid to fly again. My answer to her was yes, I was afraid, but I had to fly home the next day. I didn't have a choice in the matter.

During the rest of the Oprah show, two survivors from United Flight 811, Honolulu to New Zealand on February 24, 1989 were interviewed, as well as the author of *Blind Trust*, John J. Nance. When John Nance was asked where the best place is to sit on a plane, "it varies" was his reply.

The two survivors from Flight 811 were spouses who had been sitting in row 13. They stated that they watched in horror as the passengers from rows 8 through 12, in front of them, disappeared in an instant. There was no warning, nothing. Nine people were gone.

Twenty minutes afterward, with a large hole in the plane and the floor in front of them gone, they landed back in Honolulu. Guest John Nance stated that when the side of the plane was ripped off, the g-forces of that plane would have caused those nine passengers to die instantly of broken necks.

Ref: Los Angeles Times, February 25, 1989

Seats in and around Row 9 were sucked through the hole. Those passengers who were swept into space would have maintained consciousness for at least a minute if they were not knocked out by the force of the experience, an Air Force spokesperson said.

But one or more met a quicker fate. When staff members of the Honolulu Medical Examiner inspected one of the damaged engines, they found what Deputy Medical Examiner Mary Flynn described as "multiple small body fragments."

Ironically, my aviation lawyer I obtained after the crash had also been a passenger on Flight 811 to Honolulu.

Reference: *Deseret News*, February 26, 1989

PASSENGERS IMMERSED IN DARKNESS, NOISE, FEAR

Attorney Bruce Lampert of Denver has spent 10 years representing air-disaster victims. Friday, he was one of them.

The nightmarish accident on United Flight 811 occurred without warning as flight attendants were preparing to serve beverages, Lampert said.

"Some people who noted the time told me it took us 20 minutes to fly back to Hawaii," he said. "I can tell you it seemed much longer. Much, much longer."

Lampert, also a private pilot, works for a law firm that routinely represents air-crash victims, including survivors and families of victims of Continental Flight 1713 in Denver, and most recently, the Pan Am Flight 103 disaster over Lockerbie, Scotland.

He was on his way to a scuba-diving vacation on Australia's Great Barrier Reef.

The accident occurred at about 2 a.m., when passengers were settling in for the all-night flight to New Zealand. Many were to go from there to Sydney, Australia.

"We were at a point in the flight where things were low-key," Lambert said. "The lights were pretty dim, and people were huddled up with blankets and pillows. Then, in an instant, there was an incredible explosive decompression of the aircraft, not an explosion." "It was petrifying," Lampert added.

"In the upper deck, where I was, one of the windows blew completely out. There was incredible noise...and dust and papers everywhere. There was terror in everyone's faces."

Lampert said he thinks the accident was caused by a structural failure in the aircraft. He did not hear an explosion before the decompression, he said, and the hole in the fuselage was cut cleanly along the outline of the airline's cargo door.

Lampert said the word that one man had sighted the islands again was passed quickly from passenger to passenger. "There was a tremendous amount of relief. People felt then that even if we crashed into the ocean, there could be an effort to save us."

Lampert plans to spend a few days in Hawaii before going on to Australia. "I want to sort the whole thing out," he said.

After my segment of the *Oprah Show* was completed, I was driven back home in the same limo I had come in. I was anxious to watch myself that afternoon on the *Oprah Show*.

I remember sitting down in our living room with my family, and then seeing myself on the television as Oprah was speaking to me. What a surreal experience—knowing that thousands of people were watching the *Oprah Show* and that I was being heard and observed on national television.

9

FRUSTRATION AND RUDENESS

Later, one of the rude people I was to encounter after the crash was a clerk in the motor vehicle department. Not long after the crash, I had to get a new driver's license. I had no form of identification that I could show except a copy of my birth certificate. Nothing with a picture on it.

When I told the clerk what I was there for, I felt right away some animosity coming from her. I tried to explain that I had no current form of identity in which to provide proof of who I was. I told her I lost everything on the plane. This was the truth and a logical explanation for me, but she looked at me as if I had lost my mind. I further explained to her that I was a survivor of the plane crash in Sioux City and told her again that I had lost everything. She was adamant about telling me what forms of identification I would need in order to get my driver's license, and I was getting very frustrated and angry as I kept telling her I had none of the forms that were needed. The conversation was starting to escalate. By then, people were watching and listening to us. I asked to talk to her supervisor. As soon as I asked to see her supervisor, her attitude changed.

After waiting a couple of minutes, her supervisor appeared to stand behind the counter alongside her. I explained to him why I was there and what I needed. I needed cooperation and understanding from both of them in my dilemma. She still wanted to argue with me to push her point, and I was beyond trying to be cordial. I looked straight at her supervisor and at her and told them both what a rude person she was. That she had no customer service skills. I was close to tears. PTSD was a big part of my everyday life and moods. After my outburst, the supervisor softened, looked at my birth certificate, and proceeded to help me. (This was before we had computers that store all of the data needed.)

I left the DMV with a new driver's license and a sense of accomplishment.

The tabloids took advantage of victims that had anything to do with trauma, just as long as it promoted their magazine and it sold. My reaction to the story featured in *the Star* tabloid dated August 8, 1989 (not even a month since the crash) was one of frustration and feeling violated. I have never been one to buy the tabloids, but the cover of this one, not even one month after the plane crash, caught my eye as I was at the checkout at a local grocery store. "Miracle Baby of Flight 232" was the caption placed in the lower left-hand corner on the front of *the Star* magazine. Lori Michaelson and daughter Sabrina were pictured. The picture caught Lori kissing little Sabrina, and the bruise on Sabrina's left cheek is clearly visible. That was the same mark I had seen on her cheek when she was handed to me by Jerry Schemmel. I had to read the article!

As I opened to the first page, there were photos of the wreckage of the tail section, Jerry Schemmel and his wife, the Michaelson family, and what was supposed to be a photo of myself but was not. The caption below stated: "Hero Jerry Schemmel (left with wife Diane) found baby Sabrina crying in a luggage compartment. He carried her out of the plane and handed her to Margo Crain (above)."

Well, the caption was true, but the picture that was portrayed as myself was not. Also, the caption below the wreckage of the tail stated: "This is the section of the plane in which most of the 186 survivors, including the Michaelson's, were seated. The death toll was 111 dead." That was not true either. Many of the passengers in the tail section perished. Most of the survivors came from the main fuselage that lie upside down in the cornfield.

When I saw this, I became terribly upset, and after I got home, I called the editorial office's phone number that was listed at the bottom of the first page. I was able to talk to a "live" person and told them the mistake they made regarding my photograph.

"Where did you get this photo?" I asked. "That is not me!"

The voice on the other end of the phone said, "Weren't you at"—(I can't remember the place he specified)—"in Chicago? That's where it was taken."

"No!" I replied. "I have never been there, nor was I in Chicago after the crash!"

I remember using a few choice words to tell this person how upsetting this was to me, but he was not convinced that it was not me in the picture. After a few minutes, I hung up and realized that freedom of the press is just that. They have the freedom to print whatever they want, and there really was nothing I could do about it. However, the quotes that were used to describe my part of the story in the article were correct. It was exactly what I had said on the Oprah show.

I left it alone, but I still get angry and frustrated when I look at this article. I still feel violated in a certain way. The tabloids are very corrupt and artificial. To this day, I still feel like that.

10

CHANGE

There are few emotions or reactions that I have now that do not relate back to that fateful day when thousands of lives changed in an instant. The strength I found to get through the following minutes, hours, days, months, and years after the crash came from faith, family, close friends, and therapy. I had the sheer will and determination not to let the tragedy overcome me. Thirty-two years of healing and living since the crash has finally allowed me to be able to put my thoughts and feelings together. To be able to dig up the past and spread it out before me so that I might be able to come to some sort of closure. Reliving that day means feeling again all the pent-up emotions that seem to have been stored safely away. Like the memories that some people store away in an old trunk in the attic; eventually, they will be taken out and examined again ever so carefully. Only then are the memories allowed to return.

Denial was the first defense mechanism that was recognized. There were days that I felt vulnerable to all of life's problems and adversities. Other days I felt invincible. Even thirty-two years later, as I finish drafting this book, it's still hard to believe that something like that could have happened to me! However, to step back into my life the way it was before the crash was something I couldn't and wouldn't do. Once the first change began, many, many others would follow it. I was in an unhappy, abusive marriage, unhappy with myself for becoming someone even my own family did not recognize as a member of the family. "You're just not our Margo anymore," I remember my mother once telling me. I was becoming very bitter and negative about life in general.

My first 911 call came a couple of days after I had returned home from Sioux City. As I stated, my marriage was a mess, and neither my husband nor I were happy. I kept refraining from splitting up because my kids were still young, and I wasn't sure what to do or where we would go if I left their dad. He had been abusive to me in the past, but I was one of those women who thought that I had to keep enduring to keep the family together. One day before my husband left for work, we were having an argument. About what, I cannot remember, as we seemed to always be fighting.

During that argument, he cornered me in Molly's bedroom and said, "I wish to God you had died on that plane!"

Time seemed to freeze and then proceed in slow motion. I pushed past him and went into the kitchen to get to the phone so I could dial 911. As soon as he knew who I was calling, he was out the door to go to work.

I heard the kind voice on the other end of the telephone, "911, what is your emergency?"

I cannot recall the exact words, or conversation, but I did succeed in getting the message across that my husband had been abusive to me, and I needed it to stop. I do remember telling the dispatcher that I just returned home from Sioux City, Iowa, and was a survivor of the plane crash and what my husband had just said to me. I was in tears and hysterical by this time. No one had ever said anything so unsensitive and hateful to me before.

After talking with the dispatcher for a few minutes to give her my name and address and some information, she told me that they would have a patrol car at the house soon. In the meantime, I called my parents. My father was not home at the time, but my mother arrived at our house minutes later, as we lived only ten minutes away from them at the time. When the police arrived, I told them everything that had happened and what was said. I also stated that there had been physical abuse in the past from my husband. I gave them a description of him and the car he was driving and where he worked. My mother was with me the whole time, and an hour later, the police came back to tell me that they had stopped him in the car and served my husband with a restraining order. He could not come to the house when I was here but could get his clothes and personal belongings when I wasn't at home.

Without my knowing, my father requested the assistance of the police department to occasionally cruise past the house while I and the children were still living there to ensure our safety. Considering what I had been through the last few days, I was grateful for his love and support. As always, my father took it upon himself and went out of his way to make sure that we were safe and looked after.

A week after the crash, I returned to work. The company I worked for at the time of the crash had given me one week of personal time and reimbursed me for any and all personal possessions, including my clothes that I had lost on the plane.

One morning, my father surprised me by visiting me at the office where I worked for Bill. His visit was short and simple. He handed me a check for one thousand dollars, which I was to use to retain myself a divorce lawyer and begin divorce proceedings with Ron as soon as possible. The process took about six months and went fairly smooth. After the divorce was final, I remember feeling as if a heavy weight had been lifted from my shoulders and that I was given another opportunity at life yet once again. I was the primary residential custodian of Bryson and Molly, but we shared joint custody, so they were still a big part of their father's life.

That was the beginning of the end. A new chapter in my life was beginning.

11

REFLECTIONS AND FLASHBACKS

Two months after the crash, I was with my children, grocery shopping in my neighborhood store, when my son Bryson called my attention to a magazine displayed at the front of the store, "Look, Mom! That's your plane on the cover of this magazine!"

He held up the *Life* magazine dated September 1989 for me to see, and suddenly I was back in the cornfield of Sioux City, Iowa, enveloped in fear, confusion, smoke and lost in the seven-foot cornstalks. "Finding God on Flight 232" was the title, and on the cover was the picture of the burning fuselage, upside down in the cornfield. The belly of the crippled DC-10 was exposed, with flames of hot orange fire still burning on and around it. Flattened, burning stalks of corn lay underneath the fuselage and around it also. Inserted next to the title were pictures of three of the survivors. "Gripping stories told by the passengers who faced death for a chilling 41 minutes" was the caption under the title.

As I stood in the store, I could smell the burning fuel, choking smoke, and burning human flesh that had invaded my nostrils that fateful day. My eyes flew wide open, my mouth forming an "O" and a small cry of grief came out of me. I was not conscious of being in the store anymore. All I could do was stand, with tears in my eyes, holding the magazine. After thumbing through the magazine, I saw a couple of survivors I remembered. One of them was Rod Vetter, the man who was sitting next to me in seat 19D. I knew I had to have a copy of it.

This is the picture that was on the Life *magazine cover*

It was interesting reading the thoughts and feelings of those who were interviewed in the magazine. Some had prayed while wondering their fate, some were not religious, some had their faith renewed. Some panicked, some were reserved. Others replayed memories of their family and loved ones in their head, and there were those who were very reassuring to others who were extremely nervous and emotional. I was recalling my children and loved one's faces and saying a long, silent prayer. Rod had been very reassuring to me throughout the forty minutes that ticked by before all our fates were decided.

Many of the lives among the survivors changed drastically due to injuries, their emotional status, their current life situation, their employment, their family life, and many other factors that one does not consider until they themselves have been through a life-threatening disaster such as this. It was a life-renewing wake-up call for me.

I have experienced various flashbacks since that fateful day. Some came soon after the crash. Some others came years later. I never know when there will be a certain situation, time, or day that a flashback will suddenly occur. Any sudden loud noise or sudden movement will send me into overreacting to a situation that I would usually process normally.

I soon learned about PTSD (post-traumatic stress disorder). This occurs after someone has gone through a traumatic event in which the chemistry in their body and brain has changed. The person experiencing the distressing event may feel threatened, anxious, or frightened as a result. Your emotional and mental stability is not what it used to be. It is a type of anxiety disorder that affects stress hormones and changes the body's response to stress. Often there are no visible signs, but shock and denial shortly after the event is a normal reaction. PTSD can cause an intense physical and emotional response to any thought or memory of the event. It affects every person differently, in which it can last months or even years following trauma.

My first terrifying flashback caught me totally by surprise once I had returned to work after a week of paid personal time. I was in the restroom and had leaned forward to brush my long hair, to fluff it up and give it body, when suddenly the lights in the restroom went out. I lost my balance and almost fell forward, headfirst. The situation did panic me, as I felt like I was upside down on the tumbling, crashing airplane.

I left the restroom at once, and when I returned to my office, my boss looked at me and said, "Are you all right? You look like you just saw a ghost!"

I cannot imagine what expression was on my face, only that I had startled him. I explained what just happened in the restroom. He was very consoling and expressed sincere care about me. We both knew that these things would more than likely happen periodically to me in the future.

One example of this would be someone slamming on their brakes in front of me while driving. My heart would race, and I would get a brief pain in my head. After I caught my breath, the pain would be gone. One time while sitting at a streetlight, I felt the back of my car moving up and down unexpectedly. I froze with my heart racing, while I looked in my rearview mirror. It was two teenage boys who were crossing the street through the stopped traffic.

They had purposely leaned on the trunk of my car and bounced it up and down. It took a couple of minutes to get my composure, but I was overly sensitive to the traffic around me after that. Before the crash, my reaction to something so minor would not affect me as emotionally.

In the winter of 1990, a year and a half after the crash, I was jogging, trying to get my endurance up and improve my time for certain races I was interested in achieving that were coming up. I liked to run with headphones on, as it helped tune out any distractions and motivated me. On one of those runs, I heard a plane overhead that sounded remarkably close, as if it were coming right at me. It was very loud and sudden. I dove into the bushes to get out of its way, covering my head with my arms, thinking that would protect me. I sat under the bush trying to calm myself and get my breath back when I realized it was just a commercial on the radio station that I was listening to with my headphones on.

Still, twenty-four years later, I had another flashback. This one made me stop and stand still in my tracks and wonder how it would end. I was working near the Pueblo airport and was used to hearing and seeing numerous planes take off and land every day. However, one day as I stepped out of the building I worked in, I looked up and saw an army C-130 coming in extremely low. It was visual behind the fence in the distance. Suddenly, I was watching Flight 232, the large DC-10 aircraft coming in for a landing. The infamous video of my flight as it was coming in to try to land at the Sioux City airport, disappearing behind a building for an instant and reappearing behind the fence where the video was shot, was replayed in my head, and I was part of it again. I stared for a few minutes at the C-130, relieved to see that it landed safely. I had to shake and clear my head before remembering where I was. That flashback made me catch my breath and my heart race just as the others had.

12

DENIAL/NEED TO BE IN CONTROL/DEPRESSION/ GUILT/FEELING INVINCIBLE AND HEALING

There are a lot of different emotions that are encountered when you become a survivor of anything.

There is denial, depression, anger, guilt, needing to be in control, and feeling invincible. A person may not feel all of these in the aftermath of survival, but any one of these can sneak up on you and overcome you at some time or another. I actually felt all of these throughout the years following the plane crash, and each emotion brought out something different in me as I experienced each one.

Denial was the first emotion that I had to overcome. I think that being in shock is the buffer for denial. While in shock, you still can't comprehend what you have just experienced. It's the brain's way of protecting you and your body by slowing you down so that you can eventually absorb the reality of the trauma and deal with the aftermath on a more logical basis.

The psychological term associated with shock is referred to acute stress reaction (ASR), which can turn to post-traumatic stress disorder (PTSD) if not correctly managed. It is the condition arising in response to a terrifying or traumatic event or witnessing a traumatic event that induces a strong emotional response. Symptoms lasting for more than one month will develop into PTSD and thus be thought of as the acute phase of PTSD. Just one traumatic, major event can cause long-term chemical changes in the brain. (Wikipedia)

I received three years of counseling from a dependable psychologist after the crash. These sessions were paid for by United Airlines up until the day I received my settlement. My psychologist was very professional, and his knowledge helped me with my healing, for during the summer of 1989, I dealt with five major life-changing and stressful situations.

Before the plane crash, there was abuse from my then husband. Physical, verbal, and mental. Then there was the plane crash itself. The plane crash was the major stressor, therefore, leading up to the other changes which were divorce and having to sell the house and move me and my children into a small but nice apartment. Then, within the next few months, my regional office closed, and both my boss and I had to search for new employment.

The distressing dreams, flashbacks, and memories I mentioned earlier are all related to the acute stress disorder. These are identified as an *intrusion symptom cluster*, one of four symptom clusters associated with a traumatic event. A *negative mood cluster* is the inability to experience positive emotions, such as happiness, loving feelings, or satisfaction. An *avoidance symptom cluster* is the avoidance of distressing memories, thoughts, and feelings. An *arousal symptom cluster* is the presence of sleep disturbances, hypervigilance, difficulty concentrating, easy to startle, and irritability, anger, or aggression.

Feeling guilty. My feeling of guilt hit me when I started to realize how many passengers suffered in the crash. A few days after the crash, numerous news reports told of the deaths and injuries of the survivors. There were 111 fatalities (later it rose to 112,) 172 injured, which left 13 physically uninjured. I was one of those 13. Jerry Schemmel, Garry Priest, Sylvia Tsao, the Michaelsons, and the others whom I am unfamiliar with. I remember only Jerry, Sylvia, and the Michaelsons being among the small group of us that were standing in the clearing on the knoll before being rescued. There were others with us, but some had been injured. In my shocked state of mind, some details were hard to remember.

In the deposition I gave regarding my settlement, I was asked, "Just from your perspective now, do you think that you'll be able to deal with the crash and move forward with your life?"

My lawyer objected, stating that it was too broad a question and that the person appearing in defense was asking me to speculate on events in the future. However, it was suggested that I go ahead and answer the question. I replied, "All I know is that I'm doing the best I can. I know I have to live day-to-day because who knows."

I was asked if the crash was affecting the way that I live day-to-day. I replied, "Yes. I am living each day for what I can because death could be around the corner, no matter where you are or what you are doing. And I'm just trying to live it to the best I can. That's the kind of attitude I've taken after feeling guilty over people losing their lives and limbs. I had a problem with that in the beginning. I did see my pastor about the guilt I had been feeling."

I was asked if I felt that I had gotten over the guilt. I replied, "No." I was then asked if it had lessened at all, to which I replied, "A little bit."

Comments from friends and family, like "you are lucky, you are alive and uninjured," were meant to be comforting and encouraging but only seemed to cause me more frustration.

When I told my pastor about the guilt that I carried with me every day, and all the "why" questions I had, he counseled me to not ask questions of the Lord. Being a Christian, I could not help but ask why did little Evan Tsao die? Why did a mother of three young boys die? Why did some people lose limbs or suffer major injuries, and others walk off without a scratch? Why was I spared? Why did the Lord allow this to happen at all? He counseled me to put my trust in the Lord and have faith, that the Lord was in control of all our lives, and the crash happened for reasons none of us will ever know or understand.

These questions were not answered quickly or easily through the years after the crash. Even though I still have many questions, I have learned a lot and developed a true, loving relationship with the Lord and do know that I have a place and a reason in this life.

By this time, I had been seeing my psychologist for two years and was to continue for another year. My psychologist and I covered numerous issues currently going on in my life. The first year after the crash was full of many changes, and I needed help processing each one. The various feelings that I experienced also needed to be addressed, talked about, and worked out. I am not ashamed nor do I have any regrets for needing counseling. I am afraid if I had not had any help or support, I may not be the person I am today.

Depression. I did develop some depression after the crash, but to be honest, I did not let it rule or run my life or everyday activities. At the time, I had two young children to raise and nurture. I could not leave them vulnerable to any of the problems I had to deal with. My son, Bryson, who was ten at the time seemed to grasp the reality of what I had experienced better than my daughter, Molly, who had just turned seven.

When something would remind us of the crash, like a newspaper article or news on the television, my son would look at me, shake his head, and say, "Mom, I can't believe you made it through that."

I took them to one of the support group meetings so that they could meet some of the survivors and friends I had made since the crash who were going through the same healing process as me. It was important for them to hear about other situations even though they were still relatively young. I drew strength from my kids and avoided the spiral downfall of depression. They still had school to attend and activities that I needed to support. I needed to provide meals to eat, a loving home for them, give them motherly love, and their general well-being to take care of. I had survived, I was physically able to continue to watch my kids grow, and I wanted to take all that in.

I already enjoyed running and going to aerobics, so I was able to put more energy into physical activities. Physical assertion helped tremendously with my well-being. I did not take any prescribed medication for depression or need to consume heavy amounts of alcohol before or after the crash. However, I did not claim to be immune to depression. There were times, when things were quiet, after the kids were in bed, I did reflect on the crash and the days since. I wanted to crawl in a hole, so I did not have to deal with all the postcrash situations that I knew I had to eventually face. With divorce, moving, a job change, and various other changes in my life, it did seem that there was no end. But I got up and faced each day with as much enthusiasm as I could. I focused on moving forward and would not allow myself to stay buried by self-pity. The feeling of self-pity and depression did fade as the years went by.

Healing. There were a lot of factors in my healing process. As stated, I found a lot of healing in physical activities. It helped with the anxiety and stress relief. There were other certain needs associated with my healing: (Ref. dissertation by Carolyn, p. 96.)

➢ Frame of Reference
➢ Safety, trust/dependence
➢ Esteem
➢ Independence
➢ Power
➢ Intimacy

Frame of reference: the need to develop a stable and coherent framework for understanding one's experience.
(Reference RMN Spotlight, pp. 8D, 9D)
The movie *Fearless*, starring Jeff Bridges that came out in 1993, was very unsettling for me. After watching it again years later, I still had a dislike for it. Jeff Bridges is a good actor, as well as Isabella Rossellini and Rosie Perez. It had wonderful reviews, and the plane crash footage was very realistic. It made you feel like you were inside

the fuselage that was tumbling out of control in the cornfield, with the cornstalks, dirt, debris, and bodies flying all around you with no end in sight except death. However, Jeff Bridges's character Max seemed inhuman to me. It was portrayed as a spoof for him believing he was invincible. To be so far removed from yourself to believe that you are invincible is not being realistic. It caused problems for his family and the people around him. He was on a downward spiral without realizing it. Of course, as we all know, the movies tend to put a lot of hype in the storyline so we will enjoy it more. But being a survivor of the crash that was portrayed, I did not appreciate it.

However, after reading an article in the *RMN Spotlight* dated October 29, 1993, I began to understand more about the reason the movie was a success (it rated an A-). It was an attempt to elevate the survivors humanizing experience rather than degrade it. It focused on what survival of such a traumatic event does to the head, as well as the heart. After walking away from a major airplane crash, the main character Max is portrayed to feel free from convention and fear. He can't return to normal. He tries to relinquish the high that helped him conquer his fear.

Throughout the movie, scenes of the plane crash are mesmerizing. Just like an action movie or viewing the real plane crash of Flight 232, as I have many times, it is surreal. Throughout my research, I have viewed the video of the final approach and crash of Flight 232 hundreds of times. It is always the same feeling of astonishment, pain, remorse, gratitude, guilt, and many other feelings, but on a different level than the first time I saw it in the National Guard Armory, one-half hour after it actually happened.

It's possible some of the 232 survivors did feel like Max. There is always the possibility of going from one extreme to another. I know that I went to both extremes, and it took time, patience, and counselling for me to come back down to earth. My frame of reference was developed through three years of counselling after the crash. I was able to finally get hold of what I had been through; the crash, as well as the adversities that followed.

In a section of the "Spotlight" in the *Rocky Mountain News*, dated October 9, 1993, Dr. Bob Boyle (who was my psychologist for three years) was interviewed about the psyche of survivors after the movie Fearless came out. Dr. Boyle explains several aspects of the survivor of anything traumatic, whether it's a plane crash, a Vietnam vet, or anything similar that takes place in their lives. He stated that "one way to understand this kind of trauma is to know that it's random. The people from the Sioux City crash had amazingly different stories based on where they were sitting. If you survived, you didn't know how. You couldn't think of anything that distinguished you from the dead. The question became, 'What is your responsibility as a survivor?' How do you live?'"

I know that I wanted to go back to "normal," but at the same time, things in my past didn't really matter anymore. My life had flashed before my eyes, and I was caught between trying to move on or returning to my life before the plane crash. Even though my life had totally changed, I was impatient with the slow process of healing and dealing with this major change in my life. I was not a very likeable person. I was moody and very defensive. I had just lived through a traumatic event, and people wanted me to be the same.

Therapists say people exposed to such trauma will be changed forever, but not necessarily for the worse. They may tend to reevaluate everything that is important to them—relationships, jobs, commitments—and often make big decisions. I ended my marriage, changed jobs, and moved into an apartment with my kids, all the while processing my personal trauma.

I had bad dreams every couple of weeks right after the crash, but in time, they subsided. I initially denied that I needed any help. I just did not want to go to a psychologist or counselor. Just like Max in the movie Fearless, there were times when I felt invincible. Then there were times when I felt vulnerable. There were a lot of mood swings that I myself didn't understand, let alone anyone else who knew me.

Some people don't know what to say to a plane crash survivor, and they end up saying the wrong thing. People would fumble for words when they found out I had survived it. After a while, I didn't talk much about the crash. They looked at me like I should either be a ghost or a nut case, when actually I felt as normal as the next person. Only the other survivors that you talk to understand what you are saying and feeling. You can become a total stranger to your friends and even your close family members. When the Denver support group was formed, I went as often as I could. It was exceptionally good therapy.

Safety: the need to feel safe and invulnerable to harm.

Finding safety as soon as the plane stopped its violent tumbling was the first thing on all of us survivor's minds. Hanging upside down in a burning fuselage is one of the most terrifying and vulnerable situations ever. As soon as I released my seat belt, I started shouting Rod's name since he was the one sitting directly beside me on my right. I was in an aisle seat, so there was no one directly beside me on my left. He answered back right away, shouting my name, and I was able to see his hand sticking up from under some debris. As soon as we could move the debris, we were able to see each other. He is the one who led me out of and away from the carnage and what used to be the cabin of the aircraft that had been flying at thirty-seven thousand feet in the air.

My very first sense of being safe was when I stepped out of the now upside-down, burning fuselage into the cornfield. My physical safety was no longer an issue at that point, since right in front of me was nothing but seven-foot-tall corn, untouched. A sense of calm came over me. There was no more roaring in my ears or violent movement. There was just the cornstalks in front of me standing like sentinels in the ninety-degree heat. Suddenly, Rod's voice was beside me telling me to "walk that way" as he pointed in front of me into the corn.

Even thirty-two years later, I am very proactive. I do not put myself in any situation that I know is unnecessary or threatening. Some of us like the rush of adrenaline that we may get from something frightening or daring. I had enough of that rush on July 19, 1989. The most peaceful, safe feeling I have experienced since then is trolling in a small boat at the back of a canyon on Lake Powell. Just drifting on the water, with the high, enormous cliffs surrounding me on a peaceful, sunny day is one of my safe places. Being home, during the first part of sunlight in the morning, performing morning routines, or after a long day as the sun is setting, settling down for the evening is the other safe place. Bookstores and libraries are also a feel-good, safe haven for me. Surrounded by love, my husband, my dog, and familiar things are what put me at ease and give me the necessary feeling of being safe every day. I seek this kind of peace every day, even though sometimes it doesn't work out that way.

Trust/Dependence: the need to believe in the word or promise of another and to depend upon others to meet one's needs to a greater or lesser extent.

Being "uninjured" physically was a miracle. However, mentally, and emotionally there was a traumatic injury to myself. I recall feeling avoided and shunned by certain people. I did not want to have to board another plane and fly home from Sioux City. I wanted a family member or friend to come to me and drive me home. Since that was not possible, I wanted to drive myself home; however, I learned that there were no rental cars available to be found. They had all been rented by visiting press and other personnel. Thus, the feeling of being abandoned, avoided, or shunned. It was difficult to try to have those that had not been on the plane or any part of the rescue understand what I was feeling. The day after the crash, during this postcrash scenario, my "needs" as a survivor were not met.

Problems occurring postcrash are more difficult to rationalize, whether it is the survivor or someone outside that circle. (P. 99 of dissertation)

Esteem: the need to be valued by others, to have one's worth validated, and to value others.

Not long after the crash, some of us survivors who were from Denver and surrounding cities started meeting as a support group that was formed. This was as healing as seeing my psychologist because it brought together those of us who had been through the same trauma in which we were able to relate to each other. We all had a different story to tell, and it was interesting to listen and learn from them. During one of these support group meetings, I met Captain Haynes for the first time. He was very humble and would not take credit for being a hero. I cannot speak for the others, but he was one of the heroes on that fateful day, and I would always be grateful to him and his flight crew. He was a professional pilot, one that was able to fly by the seat of his pants while all the while maintaining control of his nerves and the aircraft under dire circumstances. I recall seeing him board the plane before the passengers waiting in the terminal. My first thought and impression of him was "good, he looks like he is a seasoned pilot." Little did I know just how great a pilot he was.

Independence: the need to control one's own behavior and rewards.

It is human nature to want to be in control of your own actions and life. Speaking for myself, starting at an early age, I have always been very independent. I never wanted to be the leader, just a small fish in a big pond. I was content to go with the flow but still be my own person. Being able to interact with others came easily because I knew myself and just what I wanted, and what my limits were. There have been various situations in my life where I was not in control, but I was not *out of control*. For me, there is a significant difference. Just getting behind the wheel of a car puts you in control of not only the car but your life and other people's lives. You are in control. However, you cannot control the driving habits of others, the ice on the road, a rockslide, or an animal or obstacle in the road. The list can go on and on. Even with your best intentions for that journey you have set out for, things can change and go wrong so suddenly.

I do overreact to sudden changes in my daily life since the crash. While giving my deposition in 1991, I referenced how I reacted to these emotions. I was asked if I had incurred any mental stress because of the crash. My answer, of course, was yes, that there is not a day that I do not think about the crash. I described the situations, overreactions to things I normally would not have reacted to. Instead of just being surprised, the feeling is more of sheer terror. My heart would race, I would get a sharp pain in my head, and my blood pressure would rise. I would try to catch my breath as if hyperventilating until it passed. I later learned that this is called somatization, in which physical symptoms are caused by mental or emotional factors. It was a different reaction than I used to have before the crash. I would overreact to any kind of violence because I feel that any act of violence, if committed by a person, is a sign of being out of control of themselves. The fury and violence that Mother Nature can lash out with is entirely different. Some of her fury can be prepared for, but not stopped. Nobody can control that, but my reaction to sudden booms of thunder and flashes of lightning are heightened. Again, even now, thirty-two years later I want to dive for cover. I used to enjoy amusement park rides with my children, but after the crash, I could not even look at one without feeling nauseous.

Power: the need to direct or exert control over others.

I had also become very hypervigilant and continue to be so. I became extremely alert and always on the lookout for hidden dangers. Some of these dangers were real and some presumed, but it always led to increased anxiety, which would then lead to exhaustion. I am also very proactive, in which I try to plan out my everyday activities in order to relieve undue stress. I was asked in my deposition on July 12, 1991, if I had incurred any mental stress because of the crash and if the distress affected me daily. Of course, my reply was yes.

I need to be well-organized and in control of my actions so that I can complete these daily tasks. Being a passenger in the car makes me very anxious. I need to be the one driving. Minor incidents or sudden movements or noises which would normally result in a passive reaction will result in ten times the reaction from me. Again, I catch my breath, my heart races, my blood pressure rises. Just being startled results in an overreaction from me. These symptoms have diminished some over the past years since the crash, but it is still a challenge to control them.

Of course, life is what happens when you're planning something else. Things don't always go as planned, and we must switch gears. For me, that is always hard to do. When I have a mindset and a goal, I do not become easily persuaded to change courses. Just like Flight 232, once the engine exploded, it could not maintain its direct course, was floundering in the sky, and disaster was the result.

Intimacy: the need to feel connected to others through individual relationships; the need to belong to a larger community.

The first-year anniversary of the crash was also a big part of the healing process. It was important to follow through and be a part of the celebration of life for all of us survivors. I was very curious to see the runway and area in which the plane crashed. To meet the other survivors who would be there and to feel a part of a celebration of which I have never experienced before was exciting. Even though I am sure a lot of us passengers were at different points in our individual healing process, we were going to gather together to remember those who died, those who survived, those who were part of the rescue responders, and everything and everyone that was a part of that historic, miraculous day. We were all gathered together in the same place for the same reason.

As mentioned, some of us met throughout the following year up to the second anniversary of the crash. On that special date, a group of us met for dinner and had a group picture taken. I still display that photo on a table in my living room, as well as the autographed photo of Captain Al Haynes sitting in the cockpit of a DC-10.

Again, we were gathered in the same place for the same reason. We were all part of a small and intimate family that could relate to each other like no one else was able to. However, through the years, I have lost contact with some of these survivors but do stay connected to a few of them.

Feeling invincible. This was a short-lived feeling that I experienced a few times. When I would have a good day, where there were no worries and things went as planned, I would be on top of the world. I felt like I could conquer and face any adversity that I was presented with. I survived a plane crash, physical abuse, a divorce, major changes in my life that occurred within a span of a few months. Was there nothing I could not do? After patting myself on the back a few times, reality would finally hit and challenge me. My children would still oppose me. There were still problems that would arise at work that needed to be tackled. There were rude and crazy drivers on the road, there were people who would get in my space that annoyed or angered me. These situations were all reality checks. I was human and still learning something new every day.

13

FLYING AGAIN

On September 13, 1989, close to exactly two months after the crash, I boarded another plane for Chicago. Before going to the airport to catch my flight in the late afternoon, I spoke at my father's Littleton, Kiwanis luncheon group.

I remember standing on the podium and looking into all these expectant men's faces. Some had looks of wonder, some of concern, some of disbelief, and some were familiar to me. After being asked to share my experience of the plane crash, I stepped up to the microphone and told my most recent memories of being a survivor on Flight 232.

Quoting from the Littleton Independent, *September 14, 1989.* "I remember the events leading up to Flight 232 when I boarded it in Denver. When the crew came aboard, I was struck by the youth of what I thought was the pilot and cringed in my shoes. Then he was followed by our veteran pilot who was soon to use all the tricks he knew. I had been receiving counseling since right after the crash and I shared some of my counselor's advice. He told me, "You have two things going on in your mind. You feel for the companions who lost their lives, and then you turn around and rejoice you are among the living. These two thoughts seem in conflict."

I had to summarize some of the experience I had due to time constraint, but I was able to talk about it from my heart, and my emotions were real because the crash was still fresh and raw in my memory. I received a few chuckles when I talked about my kids' reaction to my being in a plane crash. Bryson was ten at the time, and Molly was seven.

I told the Kiwanis group that my son Bryson would shake his head and look at me and say, "I can't believe you survived that, Mom."

My daughter Molly cried when she heard that morning that I was going to fly to Chicago and asked me, "Mommy, are you coming back?"

There was a lot of compassion in that room that afternoon and a lot of "have a safe flight" from my audience. My parting words were, "Flight 232 altered the direction of my life. My direction has changed, and I am beginning all over."

I could not believe I was going to get on another plane again to fly to Chicago that very afternoon. I guess you could call it "getting back on the horse."

I did have a successful flight to Chicago that day, and my colleagues at the home office in Chicago were ever so gracious and ecstatic that I was there. I was extremely nervous about flying again, but I had succeeded in doing what I had set out to do two months earlier. That was a personal best for me at the time.

14

FIRST-YEAR ANNIVERSARY

Before I knew it, one year had passed since the crash. It had been a busy and very productive year for me.

I was still going to therapy and would for another two years. I had been through a divorce, a major residential move, and a job change. I was also trying the dating scene out. Nothing serious, just a couple of nice men who were good friends to me. I was enjoying being single and the freedom it gave me to do things. I was meeting new friends and coworkers, all the while celebrating being alive.

About one month before the first-year anniversary, I received a phone call from local Sioux City news station KTIY. They had contacted a couple of survivors from Denver and wanted to interview us for the coverage of the upcoming anniversary. I knew there was going to be a reunion, and I was going to attend it, so I said yes, I would be happy to be interviewed. The news reporter and camera crew interviewed and filmed myself, Garry Priest and Dr. Bob Boyle (my psychologist), all from Denver. When I was interviewed, it was done in the comfort of my home, with my kids, and while we were walking along the river that ran by the apartment complex we were living in at the time. I had no idea what parts of the interview were going to be shown but was anxious to see it when it was aired. To my disappointment, it was not going to air in Denver, since it was the local news station from Sioux City, Iowa, that had filmed it.

My father joined me on the long drive to Sioux City for the one-year anniversary that was to take place on the exact date of July 19. I saw myself on television when my father and I stopped in a liquor store in Sioux City soon after we arrived. The television station was showing previews of the upcoming special of the one-year anniversary of Flight 232. I heard my voice and looked up. It took me a minute to discern what I was seeing. Then it hit me. I was seeing a part of the interview I had given a couple of days ago.

"Look, Dad, that's me!"

I had not yet seen the interview, as the news story had not been entirely released yet. Still, it was strange to suddenly see myself on television. (I did eventually receive a copy of the whole one-year news special soon after I returned home from Sioux City.) The first vision that everyone saw at the beginning of the special was, of course, the footage of the plane coming in to try to land and then the fireball as it was crashing, which was filmed behind a fence. Millions of people have seen that footage over the years, and it never fails to capture your attention right away.

Sioux City Fire Chief Bob Hamilton is interviewed and describes the scenario of the position of the plane after it broke up upon impact and how he and the other rescue personnel reacted to a tragedy of this multitude. Their own adrenaline kept them focused and going during the first hours after the crash and the next few days. News footage of National Guard rescuers removing a body (in a body bag) from the wreckage is shown. Nurses and doctors from St. Luke and Marian Hospitals are interviewed and spoke about their own way of handling what happened and the job they had to do following the crash. Many of the passengers received major burns and injuries. Some of them were in the hospital for weeks. A handful of the passengers walked off without a scratch, although their mental health had taken a 360, and none of their lives would ever be the same again.

Preparedness was also a crucial factor in the success of the rescue in such a timely manner. Each year, the county runs a drill and practices the response to various emergency situations in a county-wide plan. Hospitals, ambulance squads, law enforcement, the National Guard, and others are a part of this planning and training. Just three years earlier, Sioux City emergency rescue crews had drilled for a wide-body jet crash and a mock plane crash was exercised, even though such planes never were scheduled to land there. Little did they know that that specific disaster exercise would play a large part in the community and be challenged with a magnitude of real death and injury. Thankfully, plane crashes are not common, but in this case, it was a very large-scale crash with a large amount of souls on board, and the town was prepared.

During this special, the runway is currently shown and is empty and overgrown with spots of grass poking up between the concrete. The news correspondent is standing on the unused runway which was littered with a large amount of debris and wreckage from a DC-10 one year ago. Even though the runway is cleaned up, the memories and lessons will not be forgotten.

Debriefing sessions were given to all the rescue personnel for days and weeks afterward. Some pursued their own personal counselling for months and years afterward. Mental health personnel explained that PTSD symptoms can pop up unexpectedly, that it is normal and should be allowed to happen. Whether a survivor of the plane crash or a witness to the many deaths, serious injuries, burns and destruction that this disaster produced, a person will be thrown back in that specific moment when an unexpected situation triggers an emotional response.

The director of Woodbury Disaster Services, Gary Brown, was also interviewed. He commented on the training drills that the county performs and the effectiveness of them, especially the plane crash scenario. Even one year after successfully accomplishing the rescue of Flight 232, Mr. Brown states that there is still room for improvement. With regards to communication between the numerous services—the fire department, the hospitals, the National Guard, etc.—he felt that there would always be a better way to save more lives. Improvements for more water to be available was also stated.

A comment was made that the phone lines were tied up by the media. Of course, this was years ago when there were no cell phones or the media technology that we have available today in 2021. I personally felt frustrated with the media. There were no car rentals available on the day I needed to return home because the media had rented all the available cars and hotel rooms. I would have rather rented a car and drove home to Denver than get on another airplane and fly home.

The next segment of the one-year reunion video was of my interview, Garry Priest and Dr. Bob Boyle. Thirty-two years later when I view this one-year video, it is still very surreal to see my two kids at ages eight and eleven when they were still so young, innocent, and in my care is really going back in time.

Soon after the crash, the kids and I moved into a nice, small apartment not too far from where we had lived before their dad and I got divorced. It was close to their school and their dad's apartment also. We were doing well and enjoying life as we sat on our living room couch being interviewed. I was asked various questions about how my life was one year later and about some of my memories of that fateful day. I commented on various thoughts, memories, and feelings. My kids were oblivious to what I had been through, as young as they were. They just knew that they were going to be on television and were acting like a normal eight- and eleven-year-old. Some filming was done outside, on the path along the river that ran by our apartment complex where Bryson and Molly are both filmed throwing rocks into the river. Life had returned to normal for them.

The next interview was of Garry Priest. He is the survivor I encountered in the National Guard Armory soon after the crash and who became a dear friend to me. He is shown being interviewed in his home in Denver, at work, and asked comparable questions as me. It was obvious from both of our interviews that we were still healing and dealing with the effects of the crash that changed our lives.

The third interview from Denver was of my psychologist, Dr. Bob Boyle. He was seated in his office and asked various questions about the trauma of a plane crash victim. "Too much, too fast, too ugly" was one of his responses. "A normal human reaction to an abnormal situation" creates PTSD.

Dr. Boyle and I had three years of sessions in which we discussed my PTSD and the various, major changes it brought into my life.

PTSD symptoms are described as:

- Avoidance behavior
- Involuntary remembering
- Increased anxiety

One of the mental health personnel who was interviewed for the one-year anniversary stated that those attending the reunion were still processing and replacing our experience from one year ago. A gradual healing process can go on for years. There was nothing magical about one year later.

After viewing the whole special, I was content with the way it was presented. Included was the entire commemoration of the one-year anniversary, as well as the wonderful interviews by Garry, Dr. Boyle, and myself. My kids were amazed and excited to see themselves on television. To this day, when I watch it, I still shake my head in wonder about the disaster that we survivors survived and smile when I see my kids with me. They were so young then. It takes me back to those precious years when they were growing up, and I feel so blessed to be able to see them now, grown-up and adults themselves.

Upon remembering the events of the one-year anniversary, I have tried to place myself there again and recall the events that were most important to me.

My dad and I made the long drive from Denver to Sioux City on July 18, 1990. Upon arriving, we checked into a hotel and from there went to meet a group of other survivors who were from Denver. We decided to meet for dinner since everyone was traveling to Sioux City that day and would be arriving in the late afternoon. It was wonderful and comforting to see those special people from Denver that I had been in contact with the past year. My psychologist Dr. Boyle was there, as well as Garry Priest and a couple of other survivors who made the trip. We gathered together for a nice dinner with some reminiscing of the crash and our lives during the past year. We were all still healing but had made progress and were getting on with our lives.

Denver survivors enjoying a celebration of life dinner in Sioux City.
Right side of picture (top to bottom): Craig Coglin (seat 9-G),
Mary Coglin (not a passenger), Dr. Bob Boyle (my psychologist),
myself, my father Rip. Garry Priest (seat 15-G) is on the left at the top
of the second picture. I cannot identify anyone else pictured.

The next day was the actual anniversary date of the crash, and there was a lot scheduled for the service that made up the entire day. That morning, the sky was partly sunny, with thunderstorms in the forecast. This was different weather from the year before, in which the skies were blue, and the temperature was hot. Typical for a mid-July day.

That morning, I was able to meet up with Rod Vetter, the man who had been sitting to my right in seat 19D on the flight. We visited the runway that the plane came in on and were standing and looking at the actual place that the plane first touched, leaving a long skid mark and huge gouge in the cement. I then walked through the soybean field which had been the cornfield a year earlier. To my surprise, I found some pieces of the airplane in the dirt that had been tilled and turned over to become a soybean field. Pieces of fiberglass that used to be who knows what and a four-inch piece of broken metal, with nuts and bolts still intact that used to hold together a certain part of the airplane. These were still caked with the dirt of that specific Iowa field where so much chaos and destruction reigned a year ago. My dad took a picture of me standing in the soybean field holding those pieces of wreckage. I still have these "mementos," and I can still smell the Iowa dirt on them every time I retrieve them from their sealed bag.

While I was walking around, I came across an area that contained some large dumpsters outside a building that looked like a large storage unit or hangar. Barely visible above the top, in a dumpster with the word "Sea-Land" on it, was part of what was left of Flight 232. The red, white, and blue, which had been the color of the airplane, and a few passenger windows caught my eye. This part that was sticking up out of the dumpster had escaped the gray tarp that was attempting to cover the destruction. This took my breath away. After I caught my breath, I was able to take a picture of it.

Myself holding debris from the airplane I found in the soybean field. The second picture is some of the wreckage still lying in a dumpster one year later.

How does someone come to terms with this kind of realization? I still gasp when I look at the pictures relating to the crash, and I return to that fateful day of July 19, 1989.

As the day progressed, the weather worsened. Before the reunion that was scheduled to begin at 3:00 p.m., the town of Sioux City prepared to have some open houses for those who wished to visit Marian Hospital, St. Luke's Hospital, and the Briar Cliff College dorms. I chose to visit Briar Cliff College since that was where I stayed overnight the night of the crash, and which held more memories for me.

Driving up to the college building, it took me a minute to recognize it. I did not recall really seeing it the day of the crash when some of us survivors were taken there for the night. However, once I went in the building, I started to recognize those parts of it that I had been in as I roamed the halls that night. I found the dorm room where I had stayed with Ruth. There were only empty beds and closets in the room, but the memories washed over me. I also found the bathroom where I had taken an emotional, tearful shower that evening as I tried to comprehend what had just happened, and to wash away the dirt, grit, and smell of smoke that permeated my clothes and skin.

Washing the dirt and grit off was the easy part. Washing away the memories of that day would never happen.

As the time for the reunion neared, I started to become apprehensive as the weather worsened and the day became long and somber. Even with the presence of my dad, I still felt weary and overwhelmed. The reunion was originally going to be held outside, but with stormy weather moving in, it was moved indoors to a hangar. People began to gather in the Public Service Company hangar at the designated time. There was a large amount of people there, and half of them had nowhere to sit. My dad and I were in standing-room only at the rear of the hangar. I caught sight of Lieutenant Colonel Dennis Nielsen greeting Spencer Bailey, the small boy he had rescued one year ago. The picture of Lt. Col. Nielsen carrying Spencer would become the model of the main life-size sculpture that is among the Sioux Land Flight 232 Memorial.

Top Picture: Colonel Nielsen greeting Spencer Bailey.
Bottom: Inside the National Guard armory. The infamous
picture taken of Colonel Nielsen and Spencer Bailey.

Jets flying in the missing man formation.

The whole coverage of the reunion, which was also a commemoration, started promptly at 3:00 p.m., inside the hangar because at that time it was raining hard, with gusty winds outside. During a moment of silence, the fly over by the 185th TFG Iowa Air National Guard, missing man formation was conducted. As the A7s thundered past, rattling the hangar, I realized how low to the ground they were. That was very moving.

Various news stations were present to video the service live nationally, as it progressed with speakers Father Marvin J. Boes, Rabbi Thomas J. Friedmann, and a few emotional words by special speaker Captain Haynes. Hymns were sung, and prayers were sent heavenward. Dr. Gregory S. Clapper, chaplain of the Iowa Air National Guard gave the benediction.

A Psalm of David

23 The Lord is my shepherd, I
shall not want;
2   he makes me lie down in green
pastures.
He leads me beside still waters
3   he restores my soul
He leads me in paths of righteousness
for his name's sake.

4   Even though I walk through the
valley of the shadow of death,
I fear no evil;
for thou art with me;
thy rod and thy staff,
they comfort me.

5   Thou preparest a table before me
in the presence of my enemies;
thou anointest my head with oil,
my cup overflows.
6   Surely goodness and mercy shall
follow me
all the days of my life;
and I shall dwell in the house of the
Lord
for ever.

**A Service of Remembrance and Hope
Sioux Gateway Airport
July 19, 1990**

Joint Presentation of Colors

Moment of Silence / Fly Over by 185th TFG
Iowa Air National Guard
Missing Man Formation

"A Season for Memory" – Ecclesiastes 3
Father Marvin J. Boes

23rd Psalm

"Five Minutes to Live"* – Rabbi Thomas J. Friedmann

Captain Al Haynes

Hymn "Immortal, Invisible, God Only Wise"
(printed on back of program)

Benediction – Dr. Gregory S. Clapper

* "Five Minutes to Live" – excerpts from
a sermon by Rabbi Kenneth Berger who
was among those who perished on
Flight 232 on July 19, 1989.

Father Marvin J. Boes – Diocese of Sioux City
Rabbi Thomas J. Friedmann – Mt. Sinai Temple, Sioux City
Dr. Gregory S. Clapper – Chaplain, 185th TFG Iowa Air
National Guard, Sioux City
Captain Al Haynes – United Airlines, Captain of Flight 232
Music provided by Grace United Methodist Church, Sioux City

A public prayer service was scheduled to begin outside, with the crowd facing the crash site, at promptly 4:00 p.m. (the actual sound of impact that was recorded on the cockpit tape was at 4:00:16 p.m.). However, because of the horrible weather, the prayer service was held inside also. I was later told by Captain Haynes that if the weather on July 19, 1989 had been like the weather experienced one year later at the memorial, they would not have had a chance at all to maneuver the plane like they did (which was extremely beyond comprehension as it was), and the result would have been even more catastrophic.

After receiving a copy of the whole recorded service, I watched it carefully and realized that some interviews were given afterward, and some additional information was included. The Michaelsons, Dr. Boyle, and a couple of other mental health professionals were included in the interviews. There was also previous coverage of Sioux City being presented with the Midland Commemorative

Spirit Award that was presented by President George H.W. Bush. Another award had been given to Sioux City as one of ten for the All-America City award, as well as various other awards. Recognized and included in these awards were the Sioux City Iowa National Guard, the Marian Health Center, St. Luke Hospital, and the community as a whole. The praise for the emergency responders, the crew in the airport tower, and all of the volunteers was endless. Quite an honor for this special town.

Toward the late afternoon a few of us survivors from Denver decided to get together at one of the hotel rooms, order pizza, and celebrate life. Some of us brought some beer with them, and we all proceeded to party.

I have to admit that I ate a lot of pizza and drank a lot of beer that night. More than I normally would or ever have. It was a comfortable, happy evening. All of the somber parts of the anniversary day were over, and we were able to relax and get caught up with each other, plus make new friends with those of us who hadn't really met but had the same experience to share.

As the evening wore on, I became very tired due to the long day and the raw emotions. I also realized that I was expected to rise early the next day in order to drive back to Denver with my dad. Since he had not attended the "get together" and gone back to the hotel, I had no transportation. Garry had driven himself to Sioux City; therefore, he had a vehicle and said that he would be happy to take me.

It felt so right to be sitting next to Garry after the long day we had. We sat and talked for a little while, parked in front of the hotel my dad and I were staying in. I kept hesitating getting out of his truck. I wanted more from this man. Exactly what, I wasn't sure at the time, but before we knew it, we were in each other's arms and kissing. All of a sudden, there was a knock on the truck window, and we both jumped and quickly separated from our embrace. There was a police officer outside the truck, so Garry rolled down his window.

After the police officer asked us if we were staying at this hotel, I said, "Yes, I am staying here, he's just dropping me off."

Well, so much for any romance to continue at that time. It was time to call it a day. I hugged Garry, wished him a safe trip home, and went into the hotel room to try to get some sleep before the long drive the next day.

Even though Garry and I dated each other periodically during the past year and seen each other at the support group meetings, I didn't consider us a couple. It's hard to explain, but as much as I like him and consider him a very dear friend, at the time, we were both still figuring out our new lives and the course they might take. I was newly divorced and was enjoying being single. When you are that close to someone by sharing a traumatic event as we had, there is no doubt in my mind that that special person will always be a part of your life in some way or another. Garry is one of those special friends that I know I will always be able to contact for no reason whatsoever and rely on if necessary, no matter how much time has gone by.

The next day, July 20, 1990, came bright, early, and all too soon. My dad asked me to begin the drive home that morning. I was still so exhausted mentally and emotionally that I only drove for about an hour before I asked my dad to take over. Of course, being the wonderful dad that he is, he knew what I needed and took over. He ended up driving the whole way back that day. The trip only lasted for three days, but it was one that I know I will never forget. It was by no means closure from the plane crash, but it was important to me, and I'm glad that my dad accompanied me and was there to support me.

15

Second-Year Anniversary Dinner, July 19, 1991

As time moved on, so did our lives. Before I knew it, another year had gone by and the second-year anniversary was coming up. This time, those of us in Denver planned a small dinner gathering. The kids and I were still living in our nice, small apartment in Littleton. I was dating Tim (who I would later marry) and going through the motions of everyday living. The kids were going to school, I was working, and we were enjoying the free time we had by doing fun things.

After a year of not seeing some of the survivors, I was looking forward to another reunion. Tim and my sister Babette went with me to this anniversary. It was good to be able to include them and have them meet some of my survivor friends and Captain Haynes. The dinner was held in Denver (I can't remember where), but it was a relaxed, enjoyable evening, and a group picture was taken afterward. I still display that photo in my living room, as well as the autographed picture of Captain Haynes. After this anniversary, there were would not be any more until the twenty-fifth anniversary that was a three-day affair planned by the people of Sioux City themselves.

On the date of every anniversary, I will always call fellow survivor, Rod Vetter or he will call me, and we get caught up on each other's lives. He had also gone through a divorce after the crash. When Tim and I lived in Indiana for a couple of years, we were able to visit Rod, who lived in Chicago. He was kind enough to let us stay with him in his house and show us some of the sights of Chicago. He has since remarried, and I saw him and met his wife at the twenty-fifth reunion. We still call each other every year on the nineteenth of July, no matter where we are.

Group of survivors, significant others, and friends at the second-year anniversary, July 19, 1991

Autographed picture of Captain Haynes sitting in the cockpit of a DC-10

16

CLOSE TO HOME

You could say he died twice. That's what happened to a young college student on March 3, 1991. Almost two years to the anniversary of Flight 232, another United airplane crashed and took the lives of all twenty-five souls on board.

This report hit me unexpectedly close to home. March 3, 1991 was a Sunday, and I heard about the tragic crash just after I had gotten home from church. The United Boeing 737, Flight 585, was flying on the final leg of its flight from Peoria, Illinois to Denver, Colorado to Colorado Springs. On final approach, less than four miles from the Colorado Springs Municipal Airport, witnesses said the plane went into a steep dive and slammed nose first into a dry lakebed, just missing homes in the area.

At first, the NTSB could not determine the cause of the crash. However, three years later, there was another similar crash of US Air Flight 427. After the investigation into this, it was discovered that both airplanes crashed due to the result of a "rudder hard over," which is a major malfunction of the rudder power control unit service, which could cause the rudder to reverse any inputs, becoming jammed against any mechanical stops.

The crash happened about 9:40 a.m. Sunday. If the crash happened a few hours later, there would have been numerous people at the park nearby the crash site, and a lot more casualties. The pilot was praised for his efforts. Witnesses said that they thought he may have been fighting hard to avoid the apartment building and surrounding streets during his last minute of life. Others said that the

126

plane was so low that they could see the faces of the passengers on the plane looking out the windows with sheer terror on their faces. With such a force of impact, everyone on board died instantly, which was tragic, yet a blessing that they did not suffer.

After suddenly rolling right and pitching downward, the pilots tried to initiate a go-around by selecting fifteen-degree flaps and an increase in thrust. However, the altitude decreased rapidly, and acceleration increased to over 4G until the aircraft crashed into Widefield Park at a speed of 245 mph. The impact created a 39 × 24 foot-long crater, which was fifteen feet deep. It was stated that the body removal resembled an archeological dig. There was nothing left but small fragments of the passengers and the plane.

There were joggers in the park, children playing, and a block of apartments/homes near the area where the plane crashed. Miraculously, nobody on the ground was killed, but one of the joggers who saw the explosion said that "it physically lifted me off the ground." A young girl inside an apartment building was hurled into a door when the plane exploded. She suffered minor neck injuries and a slight concussion. The force of the impact also shattered windows, loosened bricks, and knocked pictures from walls of homes. The front page of the *Rocky Mountain News*, dated March 4, 1991, shows a picture taken minutes after the crash of the crater and smoke rising from the wreckage. There are people wandering around in the photo and a father with his two young children being led away from the crash site.

Widefield Park, just five miles south of the Colorado Springs airport, became the final resting spot for the large jet and the passengers on board. Twenty of the victims were passengers (one of which was the remains of the college student being transported to Colorado Springs for burial), and five crew members perished. A memorial for Flight 585 was erected underneath a gazebo at the site of the crash, listing the names of each victim and a tree planted for each victim also.

It occurred to me after reading about this tragic crash that those of us on Flight 232 could have perished the same way. Only our plane would have fallen thirty-seven thousand feet from the sky, and nobody would have seen it coming, and those of us on board would not know what hit us. We would have mercifully died the same way in an instant.

17

DISCOVERY

Three months after the crash, there was a significant discovery in a cornfield in rural northwest Iowa.

In October 1989, a farmer in Alta, Iowa, yielded a bumper crop buried under six to eight inches of dirt while harvesting her cornfield. It was a find that would be worth $50,000 or more to her and her husband if it were the key part that would help investigators put together the puzzle of what caused the DC-10's rear engine to explode. Various pieces of the number 2 engine had been found by other farmers in the area, in which cash rewards were offered. However, this was the 290-pound titanium fan disk that holds the fan blades that would help solve the mystery of the ill-fated DC-10.

This discovery intensified the search in the Iowa cornfields for more pieces in order to further discover the cause of the explosion. The newly harvested fields near Alta were then searched by one hundred searchers hired by General Electric.

Depending on which highway route is driven, there is sixty-six to seventy-seven miles between the rural cornfields of Alta, Iowa, and Sioux City, Iowa. According to the flight path of Flight 232 (see page 17), after the engine exploded and disintegrated, the crippled airplane flew well over three hundred miles. Always going to the right.

Because the pilots were only able to make right-hand turns, the plane flew south and east of Alta before flying around Ida Grove, Iowa, and heading north again. Each right-hand turn kept the plane flying north in order to try to make Sioux Gateway Airport, which was the only airport in the area that the pilots could navigate. North and west of Alta, the plane had to make a difficult and almost impossible left-hand turn before lining up on course with the airport. Shortly before attempting to line up with a runway at the airport, the plane had to turn right again.

Fatal fan disk found in Alta, Iowa

18

LAWSUITS

There were hundreds of lawsuits and fingers pointing the blame at more than one company, and all of them were denying responsibility for the fateful crash of Flight 232. United Airlines, General Electric, and McDonnell Douglas Corporation were the three main companies that were blamed.

In a news report dated October 1990, it was stated that the fan disk made by Aluminum Co. of America did not meet GE's specifications. Further, GE reported that the engine inspection conducted in February 1988 should have detected the fatal crack, which was designated to be about 1/3 inch wide, big enough to be easily spotted.

When I contacted my attorney regarding this news article, he was not surprised. He said he would be attending four days of public hearings in Washington with the NTSB at the end of October about the concerns of the investigation. He stated that each company is insured, and any claim settlement would come from each said company if found at fault, even if they filed bankruptcy.

During the NTSB investigation, it was important to determine the age and origin of the crack in order to determine legal liability for the airline crash. If it were determined the crack was undetectable at the time of United's routine inspection, much of the blame would shift to General Electric. If United would have detected the crack, GE's liability would be lessened.

Metallurgical tests of the DC-10's tail-mounted engine fan disk revealed that the metal was unevenly forged, leaving a small weak spot. After eighteen years of use, the weak spot developed into a tiny fatigue crack that eventually spread, shattering the 290-pound disk.

All of this information was confusing to me. I was glad that I had a professional attorney to represent me in my settlement. My lawyers were Schaden, Lampert, and Lampert. Most of their clients from this crash came through referrals from other lawyers. My father had put me in contact with a close friend who was a lawyer. He in turn led me to Schaden and Lampert. They handled their cases on a contingency system. This means that the lawyers get paid only if they settle or win the lawsuit.

A lawsuit of this magnitude was not easily attained. Each victim's case and settlement was different depending on their injuries, family members that were lost, or any other life-changing situations that this fatal crash caused. Settlement amounts varied from thousands of dollars to millions of dollars. I gave my deposition on July 12, 1991, two years after the crash. It took three years before my case was settled. As part of my settlement agreement, I was not allowed to disclose any information or dollar amount to anyone about my individual case.

I refer back to the deposition I gave in which I felt like anything but a victim. It was grueling. I was surprised at some of the questions that I was asked. Questions pertaining to my education, the high school I graduated from, college or trade schools, any previous places of employment and my job duties and how long I was employed by them, my National Guard training, if I had lived in Colorado all my life. Other questions about my birth, health, if I drank alcohol, had allergies, if I had ever been hospitalized. Did I have any congenital birth defects, diabetes, or heart problems. The questions went on and on. I was asked about any previous neck problems or stiffness (due to whiplash), back pain, emergency room visits. They even knew the name of my family doctor I had at the time.

By this time, I realized what the representative for the defendant(s) was getting to. A car accident that me and my family were in in December 1988 came up. It happened on a snowy Christmas night. We had just left Georgetown where my parents were spending their Christmas. The car was full of Christmas gifts that the kids had received from my parents. I was in the passenger seat, and the kids were in the back seat strapped into their seat belts. They were still full of energy and excitement about Christmas and the gifts they had received.

Ron was driving about 35 or 40 mph due to the road conditions on I-70. It was dark, and the road was slippery. All of a sudden, we were rear-ended. I was thrown forward into the dashboard, and the car started weaving uncontrollably on the icy highway. I could hear Bryson and Molly screaming. After about one minute (even though it seemed longer), the car stopped, and we ended up in a ditch on the side of the highway. The rear of the car was smashed in. The kids were uninjured but shook up, as were Ron and I.

This happened before there were cell phones, so we weren't able to call for help right away. However, a passing car stopped to help us, and after seeing that there were no immediate injuries, they offered to drive to the next town and called 911. After the emergency crew came to check all of us out for any injuries and to tow the car away (it was totaled), we were then driven back to the house in Georgetown where my parents were staying. The kid's toys were a total loss as well as the car, but we were uninjured and were able to spend more of the holiday with my parents, which was a blessing.

Even though that was a traumatic accident (I had only bumped my forehead on the dashboard), I did not have any reoccurring injury after that. There was seven months between the car wreck and the airplane crash. Therefore, the defendant's representative did not have any ammunition to prove that I had any back or neck injuries prior to the crash of Flight 232.

19

SIMULATING

In early November 1989, Captain Haynes returned to the cockpit. According to an article in the *Rocky Mountain News*, he flew a DC-10 from Seattle-Tacoma International to Stapleton Airport in Denver with an instructor in the cockpit. He was in Denver to undergo simulator testing and was expected to resume a full-time schedule by the end of the month. His training was required by the airline, but not by the FAA.

I understand that pilots need continuous training due to new rules and regulations, but in my own personal opinion, Captain Haynes had all the training he needed on July 19, 1989. He was equipped with a knowledgeable crew and the brains and stamina to overcome a situation that cannot be taught in any way. However, it was considered to add the technique of flying with no hydraulics to regular pilot training.

A test engineer from McDonnell Douglas led a team of engineers to program the same characteristics as Flight 232 into a flight simulator. In thirty attempts by United flight crews, both in Dallas and Denver, using the simulators, there were no successful landings. Even though some of the test pilots made it to the runway, they were unable to maintain enough control to land the plane resulting in destroying the plane. Regardless of the landing site, whether it was simulated on a dry lakebed or large field, a smooth, normal landing was impossible. Due to the thrusting of the engines, which causes the plane to "porpoise" (pitch up and down), if the plane is in a downward swing when trying to land, it would slam into the runway. If on an upward swing, it could overshoot the runway or stall. The intense speed was also a factor since there were no hydraulics to control the speed of descent upon landing.

According to these tests and research, the Flight 232 maneuver is "not worth teaching." (11/1/89, *RMN* article)

Captain Haynes continued to fly until his retirement on August 26, 1991, after thirty-five years of flying for United Airlines. It was the thirty-fifth anniversary of his first flight and five days short of his sixtieth birthday. At that time, the FAA's mandatory retirement age for pilots was sixty.

His last flight was United Flight 455 from Denver to Seattle. In a picture in *the Rocky Mountain News* taken of him before this flight, he is shown smiling, looking healthy and happy.

He was greeted in Denver by United Flight 232 crew members and at least four of the passengers from Flight 232. Also aboard were four members of the rescue team that were in Sioux City that fateful day, his wife, three children, two grandchildren, as well as many friends and fellow pilots. Bill Records, the first officer of Flight 232 was in the cockpit with him. It was a routine flight and descent for the retiring pilot. The seat belt sign was still on as the passengers and crew started to give him a standing ovation after they landed in Seattle. (The flight attendants had to remind them that the seat belt sign was still on.)

After walking into the terminal at the Sea-Tac airport for the last time in the captain's uniform, he said, "Just another routine flight. I wish they'd have all been routine."

20

Unbelievable

Various pictures of the wreckage and pieces of the aircraft were published as early as a couple of days after the crash. It seemed that every magazine or newspaper you picked up carried a story about Flight 232 and a photo of the aftermath.

I have a collection of photos that were taken by the National Guard and various authorities of the immediate aftermath of the crash. These include an aerial view of the path the plane took on impact and its final resting spot in the cornfield, the main piece of fuselage that ended upside down, the tail section, and other very large pieces of the fuselage, as well as smaller pieces and parts, seats, personal belongings, suitcases, bodies, triage areas, rescue personnel, and the cockpit that the pilots were under, which resembled only a mass of metal and wire. The pilots had been shoved up under the nose of the plane and were trapped in there for thirty minutes before anyone realized they were there.

The following pages are of some of these photos.

*This photo was taken by an observer on the
ground, only seconds from touchdown.*

*The path of destruction. What was left of the main fuselage, upside down
in the cornfield. This is the part of the wreckage that I walked out of.*

This is the tail section of the wreckage. It rested quite a distance from the main fuselage (prior picture). A few of the passengers that were seated in this section did survive.

Another view of the tail section

*The number 2 (tail mounted) engine that failed
after all hydraulics were severed.*

One of many large pieces of the fuselage that are unrecognizable.

Seats inside the fuselage. Hopefully, these passengers survived.

Smoke from the crash can be seen as rescue personnel and equipment are lined up waiting to help. Many more had already arrived at the crash site.

A single, undamaged cowboy hat rests among the catastrophic wreckage.

This is the cockpit wreckage in which Captain Haynes, William Records, Dudley Dvorak, and Denny Fitch were trapped under. They were not detected until one of the rescue workers heard a cry for help coming from this heap of debris.

Rescuers still trying to extricate the pilots

Part of the triage area that was set up close to the site of the crash. There were a few walking wounded in the area.

Near the tail section, military rescue personnel lining up to walk through the seven-foot corn in search of passengers.

Clothing, shoes, and other personal items that were recovered from the luggage that was strewn along the path of the wreckage. I never did recover any of my personal items. I was afraid to.

21

A THOUSAND HEROES

The following is an account of the crash, which, although closely resembles what actually happened, also has some fictional characters and scenes that are portrayed.

Made for television movie *Crash Landing. The Rescue of Flight 232* shown on ABC, aired on February 24, 1992. It is also known by the title *A Thousand Heroes*.

There are a few well-known names that starred in the movie. Charlton Heston played Captain Haynes, James Coburn played Red Dog, the fire chief of the 185th Air National Guard, and Richard Thomas played Gary Brown, the Woodbury County Disaster Services Director. All three of these lead roles were essential and crucial in the rescue of Flight 232. Bigger-than-life Charlton Heston still had some big shoes to fill, as well as the other two lead actors.

Being in the cockpit of a doomed DC-10 jet filled with 296 souls on board and using all of your mental and physical strength to keep it in the air is a job for Superman. When you are in charge of a multitude of people that you have to organize and synchronize in a short matter of time is another difficult job. Fighting a fire that a jumbo jet has produced in order to save lives is also a truly large feat with big shoes to fill.

If there had been no real crash landing and this movie was made based on such an incident, I would have been in denial that anything like that could happen in real life. In other words, you have to be there as one of the survivors on board the aircraft, or one of the rescuers that was actually on the scene as it happened. However, there were some crucial, realistic scenes that brought the incident to life. Other than the numerous documentaries that have been produced about Flight 232, this movie was moving and brought many emotions and memories back to the surface when I watched it.

It starts out with Charlton Heston's voice describing the soybean and cornfields of Iowa while showing a bird's-eye view as if you were truly a bird flying overhead. It gives you a beautiful sight and serene feeling while being in the air. As you watch the beginning of the movie, there is none of the fear or anxiousness that the passengers on Flight 232 felt. Then the next scene is a mock disaster, emergency drill. It had the same characteristics as a real airplane crash, with volunteers simulating as injured victims, and rescue personnel and vehicles responding as they would if it was a real emergency. There were personality conflicts among some of the of personnel in training. However, these conflicts were sidelined when these people faced a real, unexpected emergency a couple of years later.

The souls on board Flight 232 had no idea that hundreds of people on the ground were putting their skills and knowledge together and preparing for a major airline emergency. There were four Air National Guard jets that were in the air at the same time. They didn't have much time to land and clear the runway before 232 came in. All of the rescue equipment was lined up on an old runway but had to change position to another runway at the last minute, since 232 couldn't make the turn needed to reach the runway that the tower had it lined up on. Everyone on the ground thought that we were going to make it. However, as I watched the movie, the look of hope that showed on everyone's face that watched us come down turned quickly to utter dismay and disbelief as the plane crashed. The real film footage that was taken as we crashed, of the plane disappearing behind a building and reappearing before it hit the ground and turned into a large fireball, appeared in the movie. It is one of the most memorable sights forever burned into my brain and is also known around the world today. Of course, with the magnitude of the crash, nobody on the ground thought there were any survivors.

As the rescue crews were able to get closer to the burning debris, they saw some passengers on the runway still strapped in their seats.

A triage area was being hurriedly set up nearby in case any of the people on the runway were still alive. Fire Chief "Red Dog" was visible in his bright red jumpsuit in order for rescue personnel to see him and be able to follow his commands. The fire trucks got as close as they could to the main fuselage that was burning in the cornfield. Most of the passengers, including myself, who were in the burning fuselage had already gotten out before the fire became uncontrollable and engulfed that part of the plane. Some of them were not so fortunate. Solemnly, the tower announced that Sioux City Airport was closed while rescue workers were running to the victims strewn on the runway to determine if they were alive.

I was unaware of everything that was happening on the runway as I walked away in total shock, as if someone else was in my place. Rod Vetter told me to walk into the corn away from the runway. I am so thankful that I did just that. I can't imagine the horrific sight that met the rescue personnel. Some of these people were professionals and some were volunteers. Regardless, that is something that no one should have to witness. So it was unbelievable when some of the survivors were seen walking out of the back end of the cornfield. Behind them, the fuselage was exploding as the oxygen cylinders caught fire, throwing shrapnel into the air. Some of the scenes and dialogue in the movie did not fit the scenario of the real thing. A boy about the age of ten was portrayed as surviving the crash by opening one of the fuselage doors and jumping out of the aircraft before the plane crashed. This did not happen. Some of this movie hype was to be expected, so I moved past it. Then the cockpit was discovered where Captain Haynes, Bill Records, Dudley Dvorak, and Denny Fitch were trapped. Everyone was amazed that anyone was alive under the tangled debris.

The last half hour of the movie is about the extraordinary efforts of the medical personnel. Some of them were pulling a double shift since the crash happened as one shift ended and another began. The efficiency in which they determined the critical, serious, and walking wounded was a credit to their professionalism. Many lives were saved that day as the patients were given the direct medical care needed, whether it was for burns, emergency surgery, or broken bones. The walking survivors, like myself, were also given a thorough medical check. No one was left unattended. Hundreds of locals were lined up to give blood soon after the crash. The rescue took forty-six minutes from the second the plane hit the ground. Passengers were evacuated and triaged within that time. When the mock emergency drill was staged a couple of years earlier, it had taken them four hours. This was quite an accomplishment for the Woodbury County Disaster and Emergency Services. This was led by Gary Brown, the director, who made a cameo appearance in the movie. Sioux City has been acclaimed and recognized for their efforts in this emergency.

After 184 passengers had been triaged and dispatched, it was ordered by the investigation team that the deceased be left overnight on the runway. Floodlights, clergy, and honor guards were stationed around the perimeter for ethical and security reasons. Governor Branstad, who was governor at the time, also made a cameo appearance in the movie. Footage from his interview soon after the crash was included in the movie. The photo of Colonel Nielsen and Spencer Bailey was also publicized in the movie.

As portrayed in the movie, a week after the crash, Captain Haynes and Kevin Bachman (named Chris Porter in the movie), the controller in the tower who helped guide the crippled aircraft to the runway, met before Captain Haynes left the hospital. Captain Haynes was so thankful that the plane was guided to Sioux City and related to Chris just how grateful he was for his calm voice while guiding them to the ground. Chris was his thread of life during the forty minutes the plane was in trouble and said he would recognize his voice anywhere. Before Captain Haynes boarded an airplane to return home, he was met by many of the rescue personnel and members of the Air National Guard. He thanked all of them for coming (to his rescue), and they gave him a salute in return. After the plane took off, a slight wave of the wings was given to say *so long*.

In 1989, the flight and rescue crews were honored at White House ceremonies. In 1990, Sioux City, Iowa was named an All-American City, and its Disaster Preparedness Program was renowned around the world. The film is dedicated to those who died, those who survived, and those who prepared.

22

ANOTHER POINT OF VIEW FROM THE COCKPIT

Reference notes: Denny's interview on YouTube.

I became entirely engrossed while watching a video interview of Denny Fitch by Errol Morris called "Leaving the Earth," which can be viewed on YouTube. It was so emotional and matter-of-fact, that anyone watching it couldn't help but feel that they were actually in the cockpit with the pilots as they were trying to stabilize the plane, as it refused to give them any control during the forty minutes before it crash-landed. Denny was a Training Check Airman, seated in first-class on-board Flight 232. He stated that the odds are one in one billion to lose all hydraulics.

According to Denny, there is a golden rule in aviation that is sometimes unspoken. "The devil you get" is what happens if you ever find yourself in the air with minimum control of your aircraft. Don't change its configuration. In other words, don't put the flaps down, don't put the gear down. Just leave it the way it is. You know the devil you have now. If you change it, you may not like the devil you get. You may lose control of your airplane completely.

However, in the situation of Flight 232, the pilots decided to free-fall the landing gear in order to slow the plane down. After doing that, Denny stated that the plane was a little more stable after the landing gear was down. The aircraft was going 250 miles per hour, which is 100 miles faster than normal before a landing. It was in a steep descent with a sink rate of 1,800 feet per minute. This descent rate was three times in excess of the structural capability of the landing gear. All the while, as the pilots were fighting this 290-ton flying monster, they made three 360-degree right turns and one 180-degree left turn in order to get it lined up with the used runway in Sioux City.

While Denny was on his hands and knees helping to manually fly the aircraft, he had a compelling moment in which he said to himself "I have 296 lives in my hands." He could have flown on a 727 which was leaving earlier that afternoon, but for some reason, he walked right past that gate to another gate, in which he boarded Flight 232. Why? I know that it was fate that the passengers of the doomed flight they were boarding had Denny Fitch on board in order for him to be present as he offered his help and knowledge and hope for all of the passenger's salvation.

Denny said, "I found salvation that fateful day. I hope that others did as well."

To reiterate some statistics, in Denny's interview, he verified that the first impact took out the landing gear. "The right wing then dipped and ripped open, dumping 11,000 pounds of kerosene which started the fireball that is evident in the video. With the right wing ruptured, the right engine was demolished also, which left the left engine running at maximum power, which resulted in the fuselage turning in a cartwheel motion, rotating around like a pinwheel. The plane then broke into five distinct pieces.

"After the tail of the aircraft broke off, it was tumbling down the runway at two-hundred-plus miles per hour with people in it. With the tail gone, the plane was now heavy forward, causing it to come up in the air like a seesaw that someone got off. The cockpit skipped like a pogo stick before breaking off like a pencil tip. When the cockpit came to a rest among the other scattered pieces of the aircraft, it looked like a jumble of crisscrossed wires and torn metal."

The pilots may have been unconscious for no more than ten minutes when Dudley Dvorak pushed his hand up through the debris to get someone's attention. During the time the men were unconscious, the rescue crew had been walking back and forth by the cockpit, thinking that it was just a heap of metal.

Denny explained that once they were discovered by rescuers, an attempt was made to lift the debris off them with a forklift and chains. "However, the crew in the cockpit was compacted in tighter and tighter each time the rescuers tried to lift the wreckage with the chains, causing excruciating pain to each of them."

After a few attempts to reposition the chains and carefully lift the wreckage, they were successful in reaching the pilots. Denny heard one of them saying, "I've got you now, I've got you." He described that moment as "salvation."

Denny was in the hospital for quite a while and was almost "lost" during the first night. He had suffered broken ribs, a ruptured left lung, a broken arm, broken vertebrae, and other massive injuries. After a full recovery of almost one year, he took his first flight back on the job that he loved on April 15, 1990.

Later, after several years of flying again, Denny succumbed to brain cancer and died on May 7, 2012. He was sixty-nine years old.

23

Interviews and More Interviews

The *Oprah Winfrey Show*, which aired on March 11, 1997, was titled "Would You Survive or Die?" Oprah interviewed a number of survivors who had faced life or death and asked them about their experiences.

Jerry Schemmel was one of her guests.

The following was taken from Burrelle's transcripts, dated March 11, 1997.

> *Winfrey*: Jerry Schemmel lived through the Sioux City plane crash, one of the worst commercial plane crashes to be caught on tape. Jerry says it was the most agonizing forty-five minutes of his life. I understand you felt a lot of survivor's guilt too.
>
> *Mr. Schemmel*: Yeah, not only because of Jay, my best friend, dying in the crash that I survived, but probably even more so, Oprah, a one-year-old boy sitting in the seat right in front of me—in one second, he's peering back at me, smiling and laughing, the next second, he's dead. That probably caused a lot more survivor's guilt than anything else. But it—it—for a long while it hit me pretty hard. It still lingers, but—but not nearly as much as it used to.

Winfrey: Was it forty-five minutes you knew?

Mr. Schemmel: We had an engine explosion, yeah, halfway to Chicago here from Denver. A— and when the engine exploded, it severed the hydraulic system in the aircraft, which pretty much left the plane crippled and unable to be flown, but somehow the cockpit crew did.

Winfrey: And so, when the plane is crippled, is it doing this (*shaking*) or what?

Mr. Schemmel: No, it—well, it—it's sort of intermittently vibrating and shaking and shuddering, and we're also taking a right turn. The only way to maneuver the plane after that—that problem on board was take right turns. And so, we were only about 150 miles from Sioux City, Iowa, when the engine exploded. It took us forty-five minutes to get there. Each time we got a heading for the airport, we'd have to come back around. We'd take a right turn and line up again.

Winfrey: So, during that forty-five minutes, was everybody completely terrified, hysterical?

Mr. Schemmel: No, that—that was not the case. Following the engine explosion, which was pretty rugged—it was—it was a violent explosion. It was heard a, and felt. There was a force to it. That caused a lot of panic initially, but once we realized we weren't dropping, we weren't freefalling, we were still in the air, had leveled off again, and although we were taking right turns, the plane sounded different and shaking and shuddering, we were still in the air. So, the panic, which was pretty rampant initially, died down pretty quickly after that. And probably the last forty minutes or so, I—I would call the—the situation in the cabin a—a controlled panic—a lot of people still crying a—and—and staying together and holding of hands and a lot of prayers, but—but not much outward panic at all.

Winfrey: A hundred and twelve people died in that crash. Jerry authored a book about his survivor experience called *Chosen to Live*. Do you feel, though, when that happens that you were chosen for a reason...?

Mr. Schemmel: Yeah.

Winfrey: [T]hat your life—does it bring more meaning to your life?

Mr. Schemmel: It does. Both of those. Not only was—was I chosen to live for reasons—I think they're probably plural. I think there's more than one. I—I haven't figured them all out, and I don't think I ever will. The answers probably will never get—the questions probably will never get answered. And it has made me a stronger person. It— it's—it's brought me to God. It's brought me spirituality in my life, which I didn't have, which has made all of the difference for me. And I honestly don't see how peo- ple can—can move forward through these kind of tragedies without that kind of spir- ituality and that conviction to God.

Winfrey: Mm-hmm.

Mr. Schemmel: And—and he's the one that—that brought me forward to—to where I am today.

(End of interview)

After reading this interview (I did not see the video of the show) and reading Jerry's book, in which he disclosed finding God in his life, I had the same feelings myself. When I exited the plane into the cornfield, very alive, I truly felt like the Lord had given me a big push and kick in the behind. I felt a sudden peace come over me walking through the seven-foot tall cornstalks and felt that I was being guided toward an opening, even though I had no idea where I was headed. The opening into a new life. I told myself that I was going to change a lot in my life, starting with the bad marriage I was in.

As it was, I had been heading in the right direction that day. I eventually came upon a small knoll and clearing in which I saw some other survivors. That was when I was handed little Sabrina Michaelson. However, being pointed in the right direction and continuing on the right path when there were so many other paths to choose from was a constant battle in the days of my life going forward.

At that time in my life, I considered myself a Christian but did not live the Christian lifestyle to a full extent. It shouldn't take a devastating plane crash or some other life-or-death situation to come to terms with yourself and God. It was a process for me, but years later, I finally reached a positive and enriching life that I still try to live and maintain. I still make mistakes and have adversities pop up unexpectedly in my life, but I have a stronger faith that they are all for a reason; if nothing other than to make myself stronger so that I may finally one day discover why I was truly saved that fateful day.

Eight years after the crash, Jerry was interviewed and featured in "Spotlight Religion," a section of the *Rocky Mountain News*, dated September 20, 1997. He talks about his road to Christ in the article.

I also can relate to his thoughts and feelings. I felt like I was totally in control of my life, but when faced with the reality that I had survived a major plane crash, I didn't know where to turn. It was an overwhelming feeling to try to understand just what was expected of me. Was I saved so that my children wouldn't have to grow up without a mother? Was I destined to do or become someone great? I wanted some answers, and I wanted them now!

Thirty-two years later, some of my questions have evolved into realizations that I *was* saved by the grace of the Lord for a purpose known only to Him. My children didn't have to grow up without a mother, and I was able to see them grow into the adults they are today. I haven't done anything in my life that is spectacular, but I have grown and learned a lot about myself and life.

During these past years, I have shared my story of survival, my spiritual growth and faith. If nothing else, I have been able to share my rocky and difficult road to Christ. At the church I am currently attending, I have been asked to speak twice about certain topics, and I have always included my journey from thirty-two years ago. I am a tool, as we all are, during our lifetime, and I have learned to work with that tool to try to sculpt my life into something meaningful and to try to be an inspiration for others.

Through all my major mistakes in life and because I still make them, I continue to grow stronger and feel as if I can make a difference in people's lives. I know in my heart that He has the perfect plan for each one of us. We just need to find the strength within ourselves.

Jerry Schemmel is involved in and has accomplished some amazing feats in the years since the plane crash. In these, he has shown his love for Christ, his strong will, determination, and kindness for others. As well as previously being the play-by-pay radio announcer for the Colorado Rockies baseball team, he has competed in nine triathlons and three marathons, as well as several top performance bicycle races.

In June 2015, Jerry partnered with Brad Cooper on a two-person relay team. GODSPEED, the Race Across America was a three-thousand-mile bicycle race starting in Oceanside, California and ending in Annapolis, Maryland. Throughout all kinds of weather—rain, wind, the one-hundred-degree-plus temperatures in certain states, day and night, across all twelve states—he and Brad won the excruciating two-person relay division finishing in seven days and fourteen hours. In 2016, he was a member of a four-person relay that set a record for the "Colorado Crossing," a 468-mile cycling race from the Utah/Colorado border to the Kansas/Colorado border. In 2017, he set the solo age group record in the same event, finishing in thirty-three hours, three minutes, just fifty-four minutes from the all-time speed record for the event, set in 1992.

There is a documentary/movie on YouTube that is available to watch. View the trailers, rent the video, or purchase the DVD that tells the story of these two amazing men finding the strength to endure. I was amazed when I watched this, especially knowing what it was like for Jerry to also walk out of the burning fuselage of a major plane crash. He has always inspired me and, without knowing it, helped me come out of my comfort zone.

If that isn't enough, in 2019, he started a podcast radio show, which airs Sunday mornings and evenings. Called "Amazing Americans," Jerry focuses on unique and inspiring individuals who have overcome enormous odds to succeed, have performed truly heroic deeds, have executed selfless acts of kindness, have been great role models and inspirations or who have generally made life better for others in unique ways. A very motivational show that will amaze you.

One of his recent guests was Jan Brown, the senior flight attendant on Flight 232. Ever since that day, she has led a crusade as an advocate for child restraining seats on commercial airlines. Tragically, some children that did not have assigned seats (riding free), that were seated on their parent's laps, did not survive, as they were asked to place them on the floor in front of the parent's seat between their legs. This has haunted Jan Brown for years, as she continues to fight to keep that from ever happening again.

To this day, child safety seats are not required by the Federal Aviation Administration (FAA). It is strongly encouraged by both the FAA and American Academy of Pediatrics (AAP) to purchase a seat on the aircraft for children under the age of two and use a car seat or other restraining system, but still not required.

24

JERRY WAS MY GUEST

In 1996, Jerry had authored his book *Chosen to Live*. In 2001, while I was employed at Young Life, a nonprofit organization that helps lead kids to Christ, I had given my testimony to my coworkers. Working for a Christian-based organization, my testimony blew my coworkers away. They were amazed. Just as amazed as I still am after all these years!

When they heard about my connection to Jerry Schemmel and about his book, I was asked to contact him and ask him if he would be our guest speaker at Young Life. Being the kind person he is, he agreed. I remember being so nervous to see him, since I hadn't seen him in ten years (since the second-year anniversary), and introduced him to my coworkers, but it all went very well.

The following is the recording of his visit to Young Life:

> *My introduction of Jerry:*
> Jerry's and my paths crossed in Sioux City, Iowa, after we walked away from the burning fuselage of the DC-10 that had just crashed while flying from Denver to Chicago. He handed me an infant girl that he had rescued from an overhead bin after she had flown out of her mother's arms. He had heard her cries and went back into the burning wreckage to rescue her. He has authored a book about his experience called *Chosen to Live*. He has appeared on numerous programs such

as CBS *This Morning, Good Morning America, Oprah, Witness to Survival, The Home Show, Regis and Kathy Lee, The Today Show,* and *Eyewitness Video.*

For those of you who are basketball fans, Jerry is also the play-by-play voice on KOA radio for the Denver Nuggets. During his busy schedule, he also finds time to give inspirational talks. I haven't seen Jerry in ten years since the second-year anniversary of the crash, but I do consider him a very dear friend. We do share a bond for people who go through something like that together, and it is such an honor to have him here.

Jerry:

I don't know how many basketball fans or sport fans we have in the room here, but if you follow the Denver Nuggets, you're only an hour or so away from us, so you probably do a little bit, you can't help it, but if you do you probably have found out we're not very good! Have you noticed that about our team? (Laughter from the audience.) Yeah, in fact I just checked this the other day, and I found out in the decade of the 90s, we're away from that now, but in the decade of the 90s, the Nuggets had the fourth worst record in the NBA. The worst team was the Clippers, then Dallas, then New Jersey, then the Denver Nuggets. So my guess is I was not invited here by Margo to talk about the Denver Nuggets. Am I right about that? In fact, she's probably thinking, I'm going to ask him to speak about something more positive than the Nuggets—a plane crash! (Laughter from the audience.) That's how bad we are.

You know I can imagine what you're thinking here. You were thinking we were supposed to have an uplifting speaker here, a motivational guy that can tell us about his testimony, and he was in a plane crash. That doesn't sound too uplifting, and worse than that, he works for the Denver Nuggets? One thing that wasn't mentioned by Margo is I'm also an attorney. (Laughter.) We've got a real bad combination here, don't we? I haven't practiced law for a long time, but what do they call an attorney that graduates last in his law school class? A lawyer, right? If you're a lawyer once, you're a lawyer forever, I guess. Anyway.

I didn't come to talk about the Nuggets or about practicing law, or anything else like that, but I do want to share my testimony and really how I got from point A to point B, which is before the plane crash, before July 19 of 1989 to today, and as Margo said, the twelve-year anniversary of the crash is coming up here this summer. It's amazing that it's been that long. Twelve years has been such an incredible journey.

I want to share with you how I got on board the plane because it's a unique story. Then how I ended up in the cornfield with Margo and handed the baby off to her is another interesting story. What happened after that is the most important thing for me. Before the crash, I was not a Christian and had no spiritual foundation at all. Nothing there at all. My wife was, but I just kind of went along with the flow with this Christianity thing with her because I was in love with her and wanted to keep her, and I wanted to marry her eventually, so that meant going to church on Sunday once in a while. I was going to do that, but I had no spiritual basis at all before the crash, which put me at a severe disadvantage dealing with the fallout of the crash.

Anyway, July 19, 1989, I was living in Denver working for the Continental Basketball Association, the CBA, the NBA's minor league system up until a couple of months ago when it folded. We were the development league for the NBA, and I was deputy commissioner of that league. I was sort of second-in-command, and I was traveling that day from Denver to Chicago, going to make the connection there in Chicago to go onto Columbus, Ohio. The next day in Columbus was the CBA's college draft. I was traveling with my boss, who is a very good friend of mine, a guy named Jay Ramsdale, who was commissioner of the league. We got to Stapleton Airport for a 7:00 a.m. flight. We got there at about six-fifteen or six-thirty and found out that our flight was cancelled. We're on United Airlines, and they put us on standby for the next four flights to Chicago. Standby means, of course, that the planes are full; if somebody doesn't show up at a certain time, you have priority to take that seat. Finally, the fourth standby flight; now it's the fifth one overall, counting the one we got bumped off turns out to be United Flight 232 that Margo and I ended up on. So Jay and I weren't even supposed to be on that plane. In fact, we were supposed to take off hours before that. Almost seven hours before that, we were supposed to leave. I know that Margo can attest to this, but there have been an amazing number of people over the last eleven-plus years who have told me that they were supposed to be on our flight. They changed plans, did something different. If everyone were telling the truth about this, we would have had nine thousand people aboard this plane! (Laughter from audience.) You know the type, right? My dad says that's the most over-booked flight in aviation history right there. Isn't it amazing how many people were supposed to be on our plane but didn't take that flight? It was exactly the opposite for Jay and me. We were not supposed to be on that plane. We were supposed to take off seven hours before that flight. We got literally the last two seats aboard the plane.

It's a DC-10, 296 people aboard. I ended up in row 23, and Jay ended up in row 30. We were separated by seven rows, despite what the media reported afterward. We were not sitting together. We take off for Chicago. I know that most of you know the story because you work with Margo, and if you lived around here, you probably followed it. We took off for Chicago, got about halfway there, the engine blew, and forced us to crash land in Sioux City, Iowa. We came in and hit at 255 miles an hour, and we dropped; I didn't find this out until a couple of years ago, we dropped about 2,100 feet the last minute. We had a severe drop just to get to the ground, to get a chance to get to the airport. I know that she has told you this, but the fact that we stayed in the air and got to the airport and had a chance to land is nothing but a miracle. It does not add up physically, folks, that we were able to stay in the air and get that plane to Sioux City. We, I had nothing to do with it (laughter). I'm in the back praying, or what I think is praying. It's the cockpit crew that's doing that, but they got us to Sioux City and gave us a chance to land, and that in itself, and I won't go into details about that, is really miraculous.

Jerry proceeded to tell his minute-by-minute recollection of the crash and how he was able to exit the plane after releasing his seat belt and falling to be able to walk along the ceiling of the airplane. After walking through the smoke and chaos, he eventually found a hole but didn't know if it was the front or the back of the airplane. He stayed inside the burning fuselage for a couple of minutes to help. That was all that was possible since there was fire and smoke all around. After he had exited the plane, he paused because he had heard a baby crying inside the burning fuselage. Every time the story is told, or he is introduced, he feels that people tend to overplay his being a hero. He referenced talking a lot about it in his book *Chosen to Live* and his current struggles with it. The "hero" tag put upon him felt artificial right after the story of Sabrina's rescue, and he still feels like it is artificial today. He doesn't try to downplay what he did, or be humble about it, he just explains that he didn't stand there and weigh the risks of trying to find the baby and rescue it. He finds himself back inside the plane on all fours, trying to follow the cries and was able to hone in on it. He realized that the cries were coming from inside an overhead bin. This bin was at the back of the plane. He later found out that baby Sabrina had been put on the floor of the airplane between her mother's feet. She and her family had been sitting in row 11, which means that Sabrina was thrown at least ten or fifteen rows on impact and miraculously ended up inside an overhead bin.

The bin was still intact, and being upside down, Jerry was doing everything backward. He finally was able to unlatch the bin and open it in order to scoop the baby up with one arm. As soon as he held her, she stopped crying. He confesses that he did something at that point that he had no idea why he did it. He closed the overhead bin and made sure that it was latched. (Laughter from audience.) He said that he had been embarrassed for a long time doing that but finally admitted it. It was automatic for him to follow through and close the bin. Many years of flying had taught him that. He emphasized that rescuing the baby was just a human reaction. However, when he did step out of the burning plane a second time, he did take off running away from it, afraid that it might explode.

After putting some distance between himself and the wreckage, he stopped to check out the baby. He hadn't really looked at her yet and thought that maybe she was dead, since she wasn't crying. After holding her out in front of himself, he realized that she was fine. She was conscious and awake and had a small cut on her face below her left eye. He took his sleeve and wiped the small amount of blood away. He also noticed that she had lost her diaper and didn't want her to get too excited (laughter), so when he came to the group of us standing on the knoll, he spotted me and handed her to me. Still amazed that she had survived, he told me that he didn't know where her parents were and asked me if I would take her.

I said "sure."

He admitted that he had completely forgotten about the baby until about midnight that night. The episode came rushing back to his memory that night after he saw her on television. He told us that he exchanged e-mails with Sabrina, who is twelve years old now. She doesn't have any recollection of the crash but does know all about her rescue by Jerry, about my role in it, and has read his book. Sabrina's whole family; her mother, father, and two older brothers survived also. He stated that the whole family was currently doing well.

As Jerry continued to talk to his audience at Young Life, he stated that he felt that the plane crash itself was the easy part. "*The most difficult part was the aftermath and dealing with the emotional trauma.*" The "psychological fall out" he called it.

In remembering about a week after the crash, he explains what happened when a trauma counselor came to his place of employment. There were eight employees in the CBA office at the time (Jay Ramsdale would have been nine). Jerry was taken aside by the trauma counselor following his advice about the grieving process to Jerry's coworkers. He wanted to explain and warn Jerry about the signs of post-traumatic stress disorder (PTSD). Survivor's guilt, anger, listlessness, and depression were all things that he was going to go through being a survivor. (In Jerry's case, he dealt with the death of his best friend Jay and the memory of the little boy that was sitting in front of him on that plane who didn't survive. One minute, the little boy was smiling, and the next, he had been catapulted through the plane as it was crashing.) Statistics show that 99 percent of survivors go through some kind of depression.

The counselor told Jerry that all of these were normal reactions that he will go through. Jerry admits that he was certain that he was that 1 percent who wouldn't suffer any of those reactions. *"Those things happen to other people. I was a tough, born and raised Midwestern boy. If you fall down, you pick yourself up. If you have a problem, you move forward, you find a solution. You don't need any help. You don't get depressed. That stuff happens to weak people."*

However, following the days, weeks, and months after the crash, Jerry did suffer all of the emotions that he was warned about. Ten months after the crash, he realized he was on a fast, downward spiral that he could not stop. All he could think about was the crash. His marriage and family relationships were weakened and suffering. Then ten months to the day of the crash, he sat himself down in a chair in his bedroom and realized for the first time that he had been knocked down and could not pick himself up. He couldn't do it anymore. In reflecting upon his wife's Christianity, and her strength and her faith, he figured he couldn't go down any further. He was at rock-bottom. The only way was up. So he closed his eyes and said a simple prayer asking God to come into his life and give him some relief and reprieve. He was asking God to give him something to hold onto, something to battle the effects of the crash with. After a few seconds, he said that he felt an overwhelming feeling come over his whole body. That feeling said to him that because of the ally he had invited into his life, eventually he was going to win every battle. He didn't realize that God was all he needed because that was all he had left.

Certain scriptures came to his mind: *Ephesians 2:8: "For by grace are you saved through faith, and that not of yourselves; it is the gift of God." John 3:16: "For God so loved the world, that he gave his only begotten Son, that whosoever believeth in him should not perish, but have everlasting life."*

Jerry: "We all pray the prayer of sinners. Personally, this adversity that came into my life challenged my faith. Christianity is not a comfortable ride, but it is easier if we have faith and Christ in our lives. I share my story with people who ask. If they are not believers, then I hope that my story will help them in some way. It opens up a lot of questions. The answers are in the Bible. The gift of grace is free to those asking. They only have to believe. I know now that if I am ever in another plane crash, or fatal accident, I know that my salvation is intact, and I know where I am going."

Before closing, Jerry testified that since he became a Christian, his life has been an amazing ride. That Jesus turned his life upside down (in a positive way) and that he doesn't want to go right side up again. All of us survivors were put through the journey of Flight 232 for a reason, and hopefully, the majority of us hold onto something positive in our lives because of it. He stated that he started reading the Bible and discussed it with his wife. That fact was the beginning for him, that he built from there. He had asked himself the same question that my father had asked me: "If I had died in that crash, where would I be?"

The group at Young Life was very receptive to his testimony. Kind, wonderful things were said about him and his testimony. All of us who were present were uplifted and amazed at his story. Even me. He stayed afterward and answered various questions some people had and gave me an autographed copy of his book before he left.

25

INSPIRATION FROM CAPTAIN HAYNES

Another person that has inspired myself and many others is Captain Haynes.

On October 21, 1999, ten years, three months, and two days since the crash of United 232, Captain Haynes was in Colorado Springs, Colorado, and only blocks away from where I worked at the time. He was there to speak about the need to be prepared for disasters. He had been doing this across the nation for the past decade, and by his count, he made the presentation about 1,200 times. I learned three weeks prior to his coming that he would be coming to Colorado, and when I heard that he was coming to Colorado Springs, I was determined to be there to see him and to hear him speak. I was joined by a fellow coworker who lost two relatives in the Swissair airline crash off Nova Scotia in September 1998. This was important for her to hear as well, as she was still healing after losing her relatives recently in an airline crash.

When we arrived at the Antlers Adam's Mark Hotel, where Captain Haynes was speaking, I saw my fellow friend and survivor, Garry Priest. I can't remember how long it had been since I had last seen him, since I had remarried and moved a couple of times since 1989. He was with a beautiful woman who he introduced as his wife. I was surprised but happy for him, and glad to see him, since there were no other survivors of Flight 232 there that I recognized.

Captain Haynes knew that Garry and I were in the audience, since we were able to say hello to him before he began his presentation. At some point, he stopped to introduce Garry and myself.

During his introduction, he choked up. "I give this talk all the time," he said, "but it's not often survivors are in the audience."

I remember choking up also when he said that. I could feel my coworker looking at me with mixed emotions on her face, happiness that I had survived and sadness for the relatives that she lost.

As part of his presentation, according to Captain Haynes, there were five important factors involved that came into play as soon as he knew that the aircraft was in trouble: luck, communication, preparation, execution, and cooperation.

Luck. Luck is defined as the good or bad things that happen by chance or someone's good fortune.

Flight 232 did not happen by chance, nor was it anyone's good fortune. A lot of circumstances were involved in building up to that day, hour, minute and second that the aircraft became crippled. The maintenance and performance history of the aircraft, the hours recorded that it had flown, the weather that day, the crew assigned to that aircraft, the souls on board all contributed to the disaster and its outcome.

Excerpts from article written by Captain Alfred C. Haynes, from AirDisaster.com:

Captain Haynes:
EVERYONE WAS CONFIDENT THAT THE COMPLETE LOSS OF ALL FLIGHT CONTROLS WAS IMPOSSIBLE.
But on 19 July 1989, Murphy's Law caught up with the airline industry and our aircraft lost all three hydraulic systems. That left us at 37,000 feet with no ailerons to control roll, no rudders to co-ordinate a turn, no elevators to control pitch, no leading edge devices to help us slow down for landing, no trailing edge flaps to be used in landing, no spoilers on the wings to slow us down in flight or to help braking on the ground, no nose-wheel steering and no brakes. That did not leave us a great deal to work with.

What we did have was control of the number one throttle and number three throttle, so by adding thrust on one side and reducing thrust on another we could force the aircraft in a skid to turn one way or another. Our biggest problem was pitch control. With no pitch control, and just the slight amount of substitute steer capability we had, it is a wonder to me that we ever got the aircraft on the ground, and I attribute that to a great deal of luck. The things that we happened to try that day (not having any idea of what would result because this situation had not been expected or practiced for) happened to be the right things, and they happened to work. So, luck played a very big part in even getting the aircraft to respond.

The second lucky thing was the location. We could have been halfway to Honolulu, or over the middle of the Rocky Mountains, or we could have been taking off right over a city. But, as it was, we were over the reasonable flat lands of Iowa, which gave us a little bit of confidence in our minds about survival. I had serious doubts about making the airport at times, but the four of us in the cockpit did have some feeling that if we could just get the aircraft on the ground, because of flat farmland below, we could expect survivors. It helped to have that idea in the back of our minds while we were trying to fight this problem.

IT WAS JUST AN UNBELIEVABLE AMOUNT OF LUCK THAT HELPED US TO GET THE AIRPLANE THERE.

Luck with the weather was another important factor. If you have ever flown over the U.S. Midwest in July, you know there is usually a line of thunderstorms that runs from the Canadian border down to Texas, and it would have been absolutely impossible with marginal control of the aircraft to get through a thunderstorm safely. As a matter of fact, one year to the day later, we were in Sioux City for a memorial service for those on Flight 232 who did not survive, there was a huge thunderstorm directly overhead; had that storm been there the day of the accident, there was no way we could have got the aircraft in to the airport at all. So, the favorable weather was very important.

The time of day that our engine failure occurred was another very lucky circumstance. Almost four o'clock in the afternoon, it was approaching shift change at Marian Health Center and St. Luke's Hospital and all the other emergency services around the Siouxland area (Sioux City and surrounding communities). By the time we did arrive in Sioux City, our plight having been reported, the morning shifts were being kept on and the day shifts were just going on duty, so both hospitals were double staffed. Furthermore, there were so many volunteers from the various emergency units and health clinics around the area that the hospitals had to turn some of them away.

And, as a final piece of luck, it was the only day of the month when the 185th Iowa Air National Guard was on duty, and there were 285 trained National Guard personnel standing by waiting for us when we got to Sioux City. So, taking all of those things into account, it is clear that there was just an unbelievable amount of luck involved in our getting the aircraft there, in our having available the level of help that there was, and in our having the survival rate that we did have.

Communication. The definition of communication is the two-way exchange of opinions, news, and information by writing, speech, or gestures, including body language and facial reactions. The act of transmitting.

Communication was a large factor in the outcome of Flight 232. For those of us on board after the explosion, even though we weren't told the specifics of what happened, we could observe and read the facial expressions and the reactions of the crew who were trying to carry out their duties. Even though they knew we were in dire trouble and danger, they were trained in order that panic and hysteria did not escalate among the passengers and cause a dangerous situation to become worse. Communication and reassurance from Captain Haynes helped us passengers relax a little and hope for the best outcome. Without the communication that he had with the tower in Sioux City, he would not have been able to navigate the crippled plane as well as he did and have a chance at landing safely.

Captain Haynes:

Communications within the cockpit intensified as soon as we realized that we were in very serious trouble. I turned to our Second Officer Dudley Dvorak, and said, Dudley, get in touch with San Francisco aero maintenance (SAM) and see if there is any way they can help us in case they know something we don't. We had run out of ideas in about 20 seconds, and we needed some help. Dudley got on the radio and spent the entire time communicating with our SAM facility that had a group of experts who were immediately brought in. They got on the computers and checked through logbooks to see if there was any information they could find that could help us. As it turned out, of course, there was nothing they could do to help us.

However, the communication that was established with SAM had the secondary benefit of enabling our dispatch center in Chicago to find out where we were and what we were going to do. We certainly did not have time to call them separately, as well as SAM and (Air Traffic Control) ATC to tell them what was going on, so they monitored what Dudley was saying to SAM. Therefore, the personnel in our Chicago flight center were so prepared for us to go to Sioux City that they pulled an aircraft out of a hanger in Chicago, loaded it with emergency supplies and people, flew to Sioux City, and some of our staff were in the hospital before I was admitted to my room. This is how quickly they responded. And it was done through communications, good positive communications on Dudley's part.

Kevin Bauchman, who happened to be on the radar console at Sioux City Approach Control at the time, became our primary contact with ATC services after we were handed off from the center. He was backed up by a team of five controllers in the Sioux Gateway Airport control tower, co-located with the approach control, who worked together to co-ordinate the many aspects involved in preparing for the arrival of our aircraft.

BAUCHMAN'S CALM AND STEADY VOICE HELPED US TO REMAIN COMPOSED.

Preparation. Preparation is defined as the level of readiness, the actions taken to get something ready.

Without our knowledge, Sioux City had already been prepared for an air disaster such as this. A disaster planning drill had been initiated two years earlier, in 1987. Much to our advantage, the city was ready for us. It was expecting us, and all of the personnel knew exactly what they had to do. The hospitals had extra doctors and nurses stationed, a large number of emergency vehicles were on the scene, as well as some from numerous miles away. The National Guard had personnel at the ready, numerous fire departments had been summoned, Red Cross volunteers were on scene as well with everything they are trained to offer to victims and rescuers. And of course, the media was there with all sorts of cameras and news reporters. The infamous video of the plane as it descended and crashed was recorded by one such reporter who was in the right place at the right time.

All of these people with their different careers and training were prepared for the worst. And that was exactly what happened. They all came together with their experience, knowledge, and training in order to offer their services for those of us in need.

Captain Haynes:

How do you prepare for something like this? I gave a talk to a safety council in Alaska and it had been entitled "Crisis in The Air, Are You Ready?" My answer to that was "No. You are never ready. You can be prepared, but you are never ready." Preparation, therefore, is very important, and how did everybody prepare?

Let us start with the emergency response group in Sioux City. In 1987, they had a disaster drill; they were required to have one every three years, I believe. This is a live drill, and once every year, in between the live drills, there is an informal "paper" drill. During the live drill in 1987, the organizers pretended that a wide-body aircraft that does not serve Sioux City crashed on the airport's closed runway. The "wreckage" was off to one side of the airport so that it would not really interrupt the operations of the airport, and rescue personnel had 150 survivors to work with.

The director of Emergency Services, Gary Brown, was not completely satisfied with the drill, however; he thought it needed improvement. He made the necessary changes and began to reorganize the plan just a little bit. Brown brought in more services and involved more communities in the general area in a mutual aid program.

One very important health group was also brought into the planning meetings that heretofore had not been brought in very much: the post-traumatic stress unit. Prior to my emergency, I did not pay much attention to the subject of post-traumatic stress, which Vietnam, Korean War and World War II veterans experienced. I certainly do now—it is a very, very serious problem. The after-the-fact stress of trauma is going to occur; it can rear its ugly head any day, and in this particular case in Sioux City the response group brought in the post trauma unit right away, so its personnel could begin their operations at the scene of the accident.

So, the preparation effort by Sioux Gateway Airport and the surrounding communities was to get a plan, keep it ready and come back for another look to see if it needed changing. The organizers updated it constantly, they rehearsed it, and they drilled it, they went through it at all their meetings to see that they were properly prepared.

Preparation also was an important factor for the members of the cabin crew of Flight 232. Their preparation was done through recurrent training every year, where they were taught to inform passengers how to prepare for an emergency landing. To be thrust into an actual emergency situation with disastrous implication was a great shock to all eight of the flight attendants (nine actually, because one who was dead heading helped out). They had been practicing this procedure during the entire time in service from one month for our most junior flight attendant, to somewhere between 15 to 20 years for the most senior one, but they never dreamed they would ever have to do it. Through proper preparation by our training center, which I am very confident is also practiced by other carriers, they were able to do what they had to do.

TRAIN THE OTHER FLIGHT CREW MEMBERS TO RESPOND IN SUCH A WAY THAT THE CAPTAIN WILL CONSIDER THEIR ADIVCE AND UTILIZE THEIR KNOWLEDGE.

A LOT OF HELP IS AVAILABLE TO PILOTS. ALL YOU HAVE TO DO IS ASK FOR IT AND USE IT WHEN YOU GET IT.

Execution. The carrying out or putting into effect of a plan, order, or course of action.

The execution of the rescue of any survivors was well-planned and carried out. The rescue personnel were able to put all of their training into effect. They had a major disaster on their hands, and only the best of the best would be able to minimize any of the final results. There was a large ball of fire burning in the middle of a cornfield which was the remainder of the main fuselage, in which numerous victims were trapped. Some of us, including myself, were able to get out before the fire consumed us. Some others weren't so fortunate.

The firefighters had to walk through the seven-foot corn in order to battle the fire engulfing not just the fuselage, but all of the corn surrounding it. Only after the fire was out was it realized that not all of the victims were able to get out.

There was a triage area set up in which a large number of medical personnel were attending the walking wounded. Other more critically wounded were put into waiting ambulances and raced to the nearest hospital.

There were so many factors to consider with such a major disaster happening; yet, everyone who was specifically trained, ready, and willing stepped up to do their job and execute a miraculous rescue and recovery.

Captain Haynes:

Let us now consider execution. How did everyone accomplish what he was trying to do during the emergency over Iowa? We will begin with the cockpit crew. When the engine blew, William R. Records, the First Officer, was flying the aircraft in the Co-pilot's position. It was his leg, and the aircraft was on autopilot. Bill had about 26 years of flying experience with National, Pan Am and United.

The rest of the flight crew members were sitting there, on this beautiful day after lunch, having a cup of coffee, watching the world go by, when without any warning whatsoever there was a very loud explosion. At first, I thought it was a decompression. It was that loud and that sudden. But there was no rush of air, no change of pressure and no condensation of the air in the aircraft. So, I had to figure it was something else. I saw Bill immediately grab the control yoke and the red warning lights illuminate for the autopilot. He had cut the autopilot off, I thought, and I assumed that he was taking over manual control of the aircraft. Now, I thought, we have taken care of step one in any emergency and that is that someone flies the aircraft. We have had a number of accidents in commercial aviation because everybody was working on the problem which sometimes is not a big problem in the first place,

176

and no one is flying the aircraft. So, step one, in any training center, is that somebody flies the aircraft. That is a little difficult if you are going to be by yourself. But that is still the first thing you have to do: fly the aircraft.

THE HARDEST PART IS WHEN THE NOSE STARTS TO RISE AND THE AIRSPEED STARTS TO FALL, AND YOU HAVE TO CLOSE THE THROTTLES. THE SECOND OFFICER SAID, "CLOSE THE THROTTLE." BUT THE THROTTLE WOULD NOT CLOSE.

I thought next, now that Bill is flying the aircraft, I can divert my attention to Dudley—Second Officer Dudley J. Dvorak—and we can shut the engine down, which is our job. So, he and I determined that the number two engine had failed, and at the time we thought that was all that was wrong. I called for the checklist and Dudley got out his book, laid it on the console, and read the first item of the engine shut-down procedure. He said, "Close the throttle." But the throttle would not close. Now, I have never shut a jet engine down before in flight because they have become so reliable. This was my first experience of losing an engine in flight on a jet aircraft. In a simulator, you pull the throttle back and it goes back. This throttle would not go back. That was the first indication that we had something more than a simple engine failure. Number two item on the checklist was to close off the fuel supply to the engine. The fuel lever would not move. About this time, Dudley said to actuate the firewall shut-off valve. I did that, and the fuel supply to number two engine was finally shut off.

By then, we were about 14 seconds into the episode, and Bill said to me, "Al, I can't control the airplane." My focus quickly changed from the engine controls to the co-pilot. The first thing I noticed as I swung around was that Bill had applied full left aileron, something that you would never see in the air, much less at 35,000 feet. Further, he had the control column completely back in his lap: calling for full up-elevator. That is something else you would never expect to see in flight. But what really caught my eye was that with the control yoke in this condition, the aircraft was in a descending right turn and at an increasing angle.

WE TRIED SOMETHING THAT WE DID NOT KNOW WHAT TO EXPECT FROM AND DISCOVERED THAT IT WORKED.

Cooperation. The process of working together to the same end.

The most crucial action necessary. Without cooperation, the communication, preparation, and execution needed to carry out any action or major rescue is not complete.

Everyone, even the victims such as myself, who were coherent needed guidance and needed to cooperate and follow instructions given us in order to help our rescuers help us. Of course, being in shock enabled me to be more cooperative, to not become hysterical and hinder any rescue efforts or help needed. In the midst of everything that was going on at once all around us, there was to me a sense of calm as everybody came together to work through the disaster in order to survive.

Captain Haynes:

The excellent co-operation in the cockpit has already been mentioned, but we also benefited from tremendous co-operation between the cabin and the cockpit crew, especially considering that we did not have a lot of time to talk to them. Fortunately, for us, the senior flight attendant, Janice T. Brown, was very experienced and rose to the occasion. She mentioned later that when I had called her to the flight deck the first time, she recognized immediately, as she opened the cockpit door, that we had a major emergency. Another flight attendant, Virginia A. Murray, who came up a little later, also took one look in the cockpit and knew we were in very serious trouble. A lot of communication was necessary to achieve the level of co-operation we needed; it happened, to a large extent, spontaneously.

The co-operation of passengers and family is important also. Imagine being a passenger on an aircraft and being informed that you are going to experience the hardest landing you have had in your life; and when I made that announcement, I did not realize what an understatement that was. But I warned them ahead of time that it was going to be rough, to listen to the attendants, and to assume the best brace position they could for their own safety. They went through a horrendous crash, a tremendous tumbling that was so bad that they could not control their arms and legs which flailed about with such force that they could not maintain the crash position. Fortunately, they were restrained in their seat belts.

The passengers ended up upside down because the fuselage was on its back, with smoke and debris all around. When they finally got out of the aircraft, they found themselves standing in a corn field, surrounded by corn eight feet high. I cannot imagine what they must have felt like. But they stayed calm and they helped each other. One of the survivors started climbing on top of the aircraft and heard a baby crying; he went back inside, found the baby in an overhead bin where she had been tossed, took her out of the aircraft and brought her to her family that had been driven out by the thick smoke. This type of thing occurred in a number of instances; passengers were helping each other, and the flight attendants were continuing to carry out their duties even thought they were victims as well.

Of the flight attendants, one was killed. The rest suffered varying degrees of injuries, but eventually returned to work. Right after the crash, they continued to do their job. Fortunately, emergency services at Sioux City recognized that they were victims also and quicky relieved them.

We tend to forget that after an accident, the flight attendants and crew are not rescuers—but victims.

Emergency personnel did exactly what they had been trained to do.

Luck, communications, preparation, execution, and co-operation—these five factors will guarantee survival during a serious in-flight emergency. It is regrettable that 111 passengers and one flight attendant did not survive the crash landing at Sioux City, and my deepest sympathies go to their families and friends. However, when the five factors involved in training for emergencies can act in concert as they did in our case, they can make the difference between a complete catastrophe and a survivable accident.

Occasionally, since that fateful day, I had been pushing my feelings and experience from 232 down into the depths of myself. However, being there, listening to Captain Haynes at that moment brought them all to the surface again. Captain Haynes spoke at length about survivor's guilt and the guilt complex we carry around in wondering why we lived and others didn't.

I was interviewed by the *Gazette* after Captain Haynes's presentation. There was a half-page report titled "Sioux City plane crash survivor relives 45-minute nightmare" that was in the paper two days later. I was asked a lot of questions and relived my story of the plane crash all over again for the reporter. I found out that as the years passed, it was easier to speak about it but still hard to forget. Sometimes, it is still so very fresh in my memory. It is a life-changing event that a person will never forget. I recalled various memories when asked certain questions about that day.

I had taken the Denver to Chicago trip before, but not that exact flight. I explained how I unbuckled my seat belt, and after crawling through the debris, I waited while Garry and another man tried to get an older lady, a nun, out of her seat belt. My brain switched to autopilot by then, and I was just doing what I had to do. It's amazing the way your body and brain will function as needed when faced with a terrifying situation. However, eventually, I had to face reality. The guilt complex that would overcome me at times. Certain memories that would be triggered. I still have those to this day.

The knowledge of the plane that crashed close to Colorado Springs in March 1991, in which everyone perished, that was referenced earlier came back to me that afternoon also. There are so many scenarios of tragedy that we as humans have to face. I try not to let them haunt me or dominate my existence. I push through and work through them and hopefully learn something new from them.

On April 20, 1999, six months prior to Captain Haynes's visit in Colorado Springs, there was a horrifying incident that also affected me. I wasn't a victim but was indirectly involved due to the people who were affected and the place involved. The shooting at Columbine High School.

26

ALUMNI OF COLUMBINE HIGH SCHOOL

My parents moved to the house that they still live in when I was beginning the second grade at Columbine Elementary. After elementary school, I attended Ken Caryl Junior High School (they weren't called middle schools then). After three years at Ken Caryl, I attended Bear Creek High School for my sophomore year, as they were building Columbine and Green Mountain High School. Those were the only two new schools being built in Jefferson County in the early 1970s. Of course, in the past forty-plus years, many, many new schools have been built as people began moving to Colorado and settling in Jefferson County.

In April 1975, I graduated from the now-infamous Columbine High School. I was one of about 250 classmates who were making history that day, as we were the first graduating class of the new school, Columbine. We were upper class students for two years, our junior and senior year, as the school had just been built and opened in 1973. I remember riding my bicycle by the location it still sits on as the foundation and first bricks were being assembled. Pictures of the groundbreaking show nothing but open space all around, plus you can see an unobstructed view of the foothills west of where the school sits. There are no homes or many roads nearby. Today, there are restaurants, condos, parks, more houses, and shopping-strip malls in the area. The population has risen drastically within the last forty-six years. All of the students who have attended and graduated from Columbine over the last forty-six years are all part of its unique but historical history. It is sad for me to think about and realize why it became so infamous. There was no such thing as a "school shooting" when I was growing up. We were all hoping to get our driver's license and wishing for a car for graduation. Our world revolved around each other; our boyfriends and girlfriends, and wishing to be asked to the homecoming and prom dance that were always the highlight of the school year. We studied hard for the SAT test coming up. We practiced hard in order to make that special sport team that we so desperately wanted to participate on. The only "wrong" thing that some of the students did was smoke in the bathrooms. There was no threat from outsiders or even from our own classmates. School was a fun, enjoyable safe haven for me. I enjoyed going to school every day and looked forward to seeing my friends.

Students were reprimanded for minor things: ditching school, smoking on the premises, or bad grades. I recall one incident where I was reprimanded for fighting in the girl's restroom, but it was for a good reason!

It was a game day. I was wearing my cheerleading outfit, and I remember how handsome the guys looked with their ties on. The guys who were participating in their sport were required to wear a tie on game day. Whether it was the season of football, basketball, wrestling, track, or tennis, it was their special day and a way to be recognized as an athlete. We as cheerleaders represented the school and the athletes as support for them. On this particular game day, I had walked into the girl's restroom during a break between classes. As soon as I opened the door, a wall of cigarette smoke enveloped me. Not being a smoker, I always gaged when around cigarette smoke. It wasn't a jock thing. I just never did like smoking. My best friend and I had tried it many times, and I threw up each time afterward, so I knew it wasn't something I wanted to make a habit of.

After looking through the smoky haze, I noticed some signs on the walls of the restroom related to smoking. They had been made and posted by students. For or against the smoking, I don't remember. I just remember becoming so irritated not being able to walk into the bathroom without being engulfed by smoke as I had many times before, that I reached out and tore all of the signs down. There was a school rule not to smoke in the bathrooms or on the school premises, so I couldn't understand why it was still going on. As soon as I had ripped the signs down, I was grabbed by another girl in the restroom. She said a few choice words to me (which I don't remember) and started to fight with me. There was hair pulling and screams, kicking and tugging of clothes—a normal girl fight. The hall monitor was notified, and the two of us girls were taken to the principal's office.

Here I was, a member of the cheerleading squad, representing the school and the students, and I was sitting in the principal's office while my parents were called! Embarrassed and humiliated, I sat glaring at the girl I fought with. I remember that she was of Spanish descent, which was thought to be an issue with me. It wasn't; I was not prejudiced. I had a good friend and neighbor I grew up with who was Spanish. I would not have cared if she were any other nationality, I would still have fought back to make my point and to right the wrong of smoking in the bathrooms.

I was told that my mother was unable to leave work to come to the school, but they had gotten hold of my father, and he was on his way to the school. "Oh, no!" was all I could think of. My father was the current chief of police of Littleton. Before he retired in 1983, he had been on the Littleton Police Department for twenty-five years, the last fifteen years as chief. It was already hard for me to get dates, as I was known as "the cop's kid." How embarrassing to be in the principal's office and have my father come to the school!

When he arrived, he and I were taken into the principal's office to discuss what happened so I could tell my side of the story. I had no idea what the other girl told the principal, but I was ready to defend myself. My anger was gone, replaced by tears. After describing the incident, from my point of view, with relief I was told I was not being suspended, but if I wanted to leave for the day, I could. I opted to leave for the day in order to regroup. I had a football game that evening to cheer at.

When my father and I got into the car, I was still so upset that he didn't start the car right away. I could tell that he wanted to talk to me. With a smile and a chuckle, he told me how proud he was of me for standing up for what I knew was right. I couldn't believe it! Not only did I not get suspended, but I wasn't in trouble with my father either! That was the wonderful, understanding father he always was while raising two girls, and still is today.

I was able to regroup at home that afternoon and went to the football game that evening with a light heart and a smile on my face.

While looking through my class yearbooks from 1973–74 and 1974–75, I am overcome with so many memories. During my junior year, as mentioned earlier, I was one of the six varsity cheerleaders. We held the first pep rally in the unfinished cafeteria, since the gymnasium wasn't quite finished at the time. In one picture, you can see the drywall and the dusty tile floor that we cheerleaders lined up on in hope of boosting everyone's spirit for the upcoming sport activity. I'm sure it was a football game, as our cheerleading outfits were the heavy, long-sleeved sweater, with the short wool skirts. How crazy that in those days, when we were so young, the cold weather didn't seem to affect us. I never wore leggings while outside in the evening cheering for a football game. I remember only that I really enjoyed football then, especially if my boyfriend was playing. I still enjoy watching football to this day. I turned into a Denver Bronco fan while married to my children's father. My son Bryson is also named after a Denver Bronco from the late 1970s.

Thinking back on my high school memories in Columbine, the gymnasium is the only thing that has not been changed since the shootings. Our class of 1975 held our graduation ceremony in that gymnasium. I was a member of the gymnastic team for the two years I was a student there and performed in many gymnastic meets in that gymnasium. I also had gym classes and cheered our basketball team and wrestling team in that gymnasium. I loved being in the library, where it was quiet and where there were hundreds of books around, as I am an avid reader and enjoy the smell of and the placement of books in a bookstore or a library. The library I remember as a student had been changed through the years since I had been in school, but it was totally remodeled after the horrendous shooting of innocent students and a teacher by two of their classmates.

This is such an infamous story which was heard and has been told all over the world. Anyone that hears *Columbine* knows what one is talking about. With the many school and other shootings that have followed through the years, it has become a template for terror.

I recall the first news I heard of the shooting. At that time, my husband Tim and I were living in Indiana. I saw the horror and news unfolding while I was at work. Tim was in Littleton at the time, interviewing for a job that we hoped would enable us to move back to Colorado. He called me with the news and to tell me that his niece and nephew were thought to still be inside the school, as they were currently students at Columbine. During that whole day, he stayed with his brother and his sister-in-law waiting to hear any news. As it turned out, his niece left earlier to have lunch somewhere away from the school and was returning from lunch when the shooting occurred. Thankfully, she did not get anywhere near the school upon her return.

Tim's nephew, however, was still in the building. After standing vigil for many hours, Tim and his nephew's parents were finally told where to locate him. He had been one of the last students to be rescued. He was physically uninjured, but it would take years for him to heal emotionally and mentally. I was not close to Tim's niece and nephew, so I only heard about what happened through Tim. It was a relief to learn that they were both unharmed. However, the teacher, and coach, Dave Saunders, was not so lucky. Hearing his name was also hard for me. He had been my business teacher when I was a student at Columbine. He was a veteran teacher at the school and a well-known figure.

I will not repeat anymore of the facts or stories behind Columbine, as it has all been said and written about since then. What I do want to express is the fact that every day should be a blessing to us. Whether we rise from bed with school, work, errands, or just relaxing at home, being retired ahead of us, we should embrace the day and make the most of it, as we never know if it will be our last. Life happens so fast, and even though we think we have control of our lives, we don't. We all have hopes and dreams to fulfill, but the truth is "life is what happens when you are planning something else."

27

COCKPIT VOICE RECORDER—FORTY-FOUR MINUTES OF TERROR

After the explosion was first heard at 2:16 p.m. (Mountain standard time), there were only forty-four minutes before the aircraft crashed. The following is the radio communication that took place between United Airlines Dispatch, a UA maintenance worker, and Sioux City Approach during those first to last minutes.

Captain Haynes radioed from about forty miles out of Sioux City that he had lost the number 2 engine. He reported the loud bang and that flying engine parts had severed the hydraulic lines. After asking for emergency assistance to the nearest airport, in which Des Moines, Iowa was suggested, the captain didn't believe he could make that airport based on the aircraft's rate of descent. Sioux Gateway Airport was then suggested.

Twenty-seven-year-old Kevin Bachman was only three months into his job as a fully trained air traffic controller. He showed calm, cool intensity during the thirty-six minutes he was in contact with Captain Haynes as they worked together to find a way to land the crippled aircraft.

There was more communication going on other than between the Captain and Sioux City Approach. Everyone on the ground and in the air was communicating with their immediate contact in order to get this aircraft on the ground. Various conversations were going on at once in the cockpit between the captain, first officer, flight engineer, and jump seat captain, maintenance and Sioux City approach. There were so many "cooks in the kitchen," yet everyone was still able to maintain their composure. One can only imagine how stressful it was in the cockpit. The following is the CVR (cockpit voice recorder) transcript and truly allows anyone to be able to feel and hear exactly what it was like as the captain and his crew were trying to not only control, but also safely land the aircraft.

Captain Al Haynes was the captain. William R. Records was the first officer. Dudley J. Dvorak was the flight engineer. There was an airline captain riding in the jump seat. This is common in a lot of flights, when a passenger that is also an airline captain is given permission to ride in the cockpit during the flight. This person is not identified. SAM is United Airlines System Aircraft Maintenance. Kevin Bauchman is Sioux City Approach. Denny Fitch is the jump seat training pilot (the off-duty United Airlines pilot and a training check airman that was on board as a passenger in first class).

Cockpit voice recorder transcript of the July 19, 1989 emergency landing of a United Airlines DC-10-10 at Sioux Gateway Airport, IA (SUX), USA. Taken from the Aviation Safety Network. Source: NTSB

The reader of this transcript is cautioned that the transcription of a CVR tape is not a precise science but is the best possible product from a group investigative effort. The transcript, or parts thereof, if taken out of context can be misleading. Therefore, the CVR transcripts should only be used in conjunction with other evidence. Conclusions or interpretations should not be made using the transcript as the sole source of information. Furthermore, this transcript is made available for educational purposes, so the reader is encouraged to read the accident description *associated with the transcripts for better understanding of the circumstances.*

Captain: Ah, we're controlling the turn by power. I don't think we can turn right. I think we can only make left turns. We're starting a little bit of a left turn now. We can only turn right. We can't turn left.

Approach: United two thirty-two heavy, ah, understand you can only make right turns.

Captain: That's affirmative.

Approach: United two thirty-two heavy, roger. Your present track puts you about eight miles north of the airport sir. And, ah, the only way we can get you around (Runway 31) is a slight left turn with differential power or if you go and jocket it over.

Captain: Roger. Okay, we're in a right turn now. It's about the only way we can go. We'll be able to make very slight turns on final, but right now just...we're gonna make right turns to whatever heading you want.

Approach: United two thirty-two heavy, roger. Ah, right turn, heading two five.

Captain: Two five.

Captain: Now the _____elevator doesn't want to work. Rolling right.

Flight Engineer (to maintenance): This is United two thirty-two. We blew number two engine, and we've lost all hydraulics and we are only able to control, ah, level flight with the ah, asymmetrical power settings. We have very little rudder or elevator.

First Officer: Very little elevator. It's hard or slug-gish. Ah, Al, do you want me to slew this elevator.

Captain: Yeah, whatever you can.

Approach: United two thirty-two heavy, fly heading two four zero and say your souls on board.

First Officer: Al, now the nose is coming up.

Maintenance: United two thirty-two, under-stand that you lost number two engine totally, sir?

Captain: Say again.

Approach: Souls on board, United two thirty-two heavy.

Captain: Gettin' that right now.

Flight Engineer (to maintenance): That's affirmative.

Maintenance: Your, ah, system one and system three? Are they operating normally?

Flight Engineer: Negative. All hydraulics are lost. All hydraulics are lost. The only thing we have is the...[and he itemizes the systems that are working].

Approach: United two thirty-two heavy, can you continue your turn to heading two four zero?

First Officer: I don't know. We'll try for it.

Maintenance: Okay, United two thirty-two, understand you have normal power on one and three engines.

Flight Engineer: That's affirmative.

First Officer: Wonder about the outboard ailerons. If we put some flaps out, you think that would give us outboard?

Flight Engineer: God, I hate to do anything.

Captain: Well, we're going to have to do something.

Maintenance: United two thirty-two, is all hydraulic quantity gone?

Flight Engineer: Yes, all hydraulic quantity is gone.

First Officer: Level off.

Approach: United two thirty-two heavy, souls on board and fuel remaining?

First Officer: Souls on board and fuel remaining. We have thirty-seven six [on fuel].

Flight Engineer: We've got thirty-seven four on fuel.

Approach: Roger.

Cockpit sound: [Sound of two knocks on cockpit door].

Maintenance: Okay, United two thirty-two, where you gonna set down?

Captain: Unlock the door.

Captain: What's SAM saying?

Cockpit sound: [Sound of three knocks on door]

Flight Engineer: We need some assistance right now. We can't...we're havin' a hard time controllin' it.

Maintenance: Okay, United two thirty-two.

Captain: We don't have any controls.

First Officer: You want to go forward on it, Al.

Cockpit sound: [Sound of two knocks on door; sound of landing gear warning horn]

Captain: Now go forward... Now, let it come back. Got to lead...got to lead it...

Maintenance: I'll try to help ya. I'll pull out your flight manual.

Captain (to jump seat captain): See what you can see back there [in the cabin], will ya?

First Officer (to jump seat captain): Go back and look out the wing...and see what we got...

Jump seat Captain: Okay.

Captain: [Pull] back on the sucker.

Cockpit sound: [Cockpit door opens]

First Officer: Don't pull the throttles off...

(For the next few seconds, the copilot and captain continue to maneuver with the throttles, while the engineer discuss the problem with maintenance by radio.)

First Officer: What's the hydraulic quantity?

Flight Engineer: Down to zero.

First Officer: On all of them?

Flight Engineer: All of them.

Captain: Quantity, quantity is gone?

Flight Engineer: Yeah, all the quantity is gone. All pressure is [gone].

Captain: You get a hold of SAM?

Flight Engineer: Yeah, I've talked to him.

Captain: What's he saying?

Flight Engineer: He's not telling me anything.

Captain: We're not going to make the runway, fellas. We're gonna have to ditch this son _ _ _ and hope for the best.

Cockpit Sound: Sound of three knocks.

Captain: Unlock the _____ door.

First Officer: Unlock it.

Captain: We've lost... No hydraulics. We have no hydraulic fluid. That's part of our main problem.

Dispatch: United two thirty-two, do you want to put that thing on the ground right now, or do you want to come to Chicago?

Flight Engineer: Okay, we're ah, we don't know what we'll be able to do. We don't think we're even gonna be able to get on the runway right now. We have no control hardly at all...

Jump seat Captain: Okay, both your inboard ailerons are sticking up. That's as far as I can tell. I don't know...

Captain: Well, that's because we're steering. We're turning maximum turn right now.

Jump seat Captain: Tell me. Tell what you want, and I'll help you.

Captain: Right throttle. Close one, put two up. What we need is elevator control. And I don't know how to get it.

Jump seat Captain: Okay, ah...

Flight Engineer: Roger, we need any help we can get from SAM, as far as what to do with this. We don't have anything. We don't [know] what to do. We're having a hard time controlling it. We're descending. We're down to seventeen thousand feet. We have...ah hardly any control whatsoever.

Captain: The only help you can get is the autopilot and I tried that, and it won't work.

Jump seat Captain: It won't work. Okay...

Captain: Go ahead and try it again. Pull back, pull back, pull back.

Dispatch: Okay, copy that, two thirty-two. San Fran [is on the] line. Give 'em all the help you can. We'll get you expedited handling into Chicago put you on the ground as soon as we can...

Captain: You want full aileron and full elevator. No, no, no, no, no, not yet. Wait a minute. Wait 'til it levels off. Now go.

Flight Engineer: Well, we can't make Chicago. We're gonna have to land somewhere out here, probably in a field.

Captain: How're they doin' on the evacuation?

Jump seat Captain: They're putting things away, but they're not in any big hurry.

Maintenance: United two thirty-two, we [understand that you] have to land the nearest airport, the nearest airport. Ah, I'm trying to find out where you've lost all three hydraulic systems.

Captain: Well, they better hurry. We're gonna have to ditch, I think.

Jump seat Captain: Yeah.

Captain: Okay.

Cockpit sound: [Sound of knock on door]

Captain: I don't think we're going to make the airport.

First Officer: No. We got not hydraulics at all.

Cockpit sound: [Sound of landing gear warning horn]

Jump seat Captain: Get this thing down. We're in trouble...

Flight Engineer to Maintenance: That is affirmative. We have lost all three hydraulic systems. We have no quantity and no pressure on any hydraulic system...

Captain to Sioux City Approach: Sir, we have no hydraulic fluid, which means we have no elevator control, almost none, and very little aileron control. I have serious doubts about making the airport. Have you got someplace near there, ah, that we might be able to ditch? Unless we get control of this airplane, we're gonna put it down wherever it happens to be.

Maintenance: Ah, United two thirty-two, you have lost all manual flight control systems?

Flight Engineer: That's apparently true.

Maintenance: United two thirty-two, ah, in the flight manual [on page] sixty?

Captain: Gotta put some flaps and see if that'll help.

Flight Engineer to Maintenance: I am on sixty-three.

First Officer: You want them now?

Captain: What the hell. Let's do it. We can't get any worse than we are...

First Officer: Slats are out?

Jump seat Captain: No, you don't have any slats.

Captain: We don't have any hydraulics, so we're not going to get anything.

Sioux City Approach: United two thirty-two heavy, can you hold that present heading, sir?

Captain: This is Sioux City, Iowa. That's where we're headed.

Captain: Where's the airport now for [United] two thirty-two? We're turning around in circles.

Jump seat Captain: You get on number one and ask them where we are.

Captain: Where's the airport to us now, as we come spinning down here?

Sioux City Approach: United two thirty-two heavy, Sioux City airport is about twelve o'clock and three six miles.

Captain: Okay. We're trying to go straight. We're not havin' much luck.

Jump seat Captain: All right, I got you one seven hundred on the squawk, so they can track ya [on radar].

First Officer: He's got us on radar.

Captain: As soon as the nose starts up, we have to push forward on the yoke.

Jump seat Captain: We got nothing on number two, number two [engine]?

Captain: No, no, we got it shut down.

Maintenance: United two thirty-two, I'm getting contact with flight ops right now. Standby please.

Captain: I want a heading of about three zero zero. We kinda got level flight back again.

Jump seat Captain: Okay, if you got denser air, you should [get level flight back again]. Whatever you got, you got.

Captain: A little better.

Jump seat Captain: Okay, ah, let me see…

Captain: [Laughs] We didn't do this thing on my last [performance check in a simulator].

Cockpit sound: [Laughter]

First Officer: No.

Captain: [I] poured coffee all over…it's just coffee. We'll get this thing on the ground. Don't worry about it.

First Officer: It seems controllable, doesn't it, Al?

Jump seat Captain: Yeah. The lower you get the more dense that air is [and] the better your shots. Okay?

Captain: I'll tell ya what we need. We're puttin' this thing into Sioux City. Get me…

Captain: Sioux City, United two thirty-two, could you give us please your ILS frequency, the heading and length of the runway?

Sioux City Approach: United two thirty-two heavy, affirmative. The localizer frequency is one zero nine point three and you're currently about thirty-five miles to north-east. It'll take about {heading} two two three five two four zero heading to join it.

Maintenance: United two thirty-two, this is Sam.

Cockpit sound: [Sound of landing gear warning]

Flight Engineer: Sam, two thirty-two. We're gonna try and put into Sioux City.

Dispatch: Sam, this is dispatch. I haven't been able to copy two thirty-two. We're hearing a rumor that he's on approach to Sioux City airport. Last we heard he's at seventeen thousand feet and he may be too low for us to maintain contact with him. Go ahead…

Sioux City Approach: United two thirty-two, understand you are gonna try to make it into Sioux City. There's no airport out that way that way that can accommodate you, sir.

Captain: Okay, we'll head for Sioux City. We got a little bit of control back now. How long [is] your runway?

Flight Engineer: Two thirty-two is very busy right now. We're tryin' to go into Sioux City. We'll call you as soon as I can...

Sioux City Approach: Two thirty-two heavy, the airport, the runway is nine thousand feet long...

Maintenance: He has no control. He's using that kind of sink rate, I believe. This is what he's doing. He's got his hands full for sure.

Captain: Okay, thank you.

Captain: You're a little more... Let's see if you can make a left turn.

Jump seat Captain: Left turn. All right. Your speed is what? I'm worried about [it]. I don't want to stop you.

Flight Engineer: You want a no flap-no slat [landing], right?

Captain: Yeah. Ah, start dumpin' [fuel] will ya? Just hit the quick dump. Let's get the weight down as low as {we} can...

Flight Engineer: I didn't have time to think about that.

Captain: Try not to lose any more [altitude] than we have to.

First Officer: What? Altitude?

Captain: Yeah.

First Officer: Okay. Go ahead and dump.

Jump seat Captain: He's got his weight. He's got his weight. He's only got about a thousand pounds to go.

First Officer: Okay.

Jump seat Captain: This thing seems to want to go right more than it wants to go left, doesn't it?

Sioux City Approach: United two thirty-two, did you get the souls on board count?

Captain: What did you have for a count of people?

Captain: [Let me] tell you, right now we don't even have time to call the gal...

Flight Engineer: Ah, two ninety-two.

Sioux City Approach: Roger.

Captain: Ease all the power back.

Jump seat Captain: Okay, the nose is coming up.

Maintenance: All hydraulic systems are gone...

Sioux City Approach: Okay, thank you.

First Officer: Yeah, we're goin' up.

Captain: Yeah, I know it. I'm pushin' with all I got.

Jump seat Captain: Power's coming back. Power's coming back...

Captain: As soon as it starts to come back... Okay, come back...

Jump seat Captain: Power's coming back in...

Captain: Bring [turn] it to the right with the right one. You got to go left. We just keep turnin' right. Still turnin' right...

Jump seat Captain: That's what I'm tryin' to do...

Captain: Two thirty-two, we're just gonna have to keep turnin' right. There's not much we can do about [turning] left. We'll try to come back around to the heading...

First Officer: Is this Sioux City down to the right?

Captain: That's Sioux City.

Sioux City Approach: United two thirty-two, roger. Need you on about a two-three-five heading, Sir, if you can manage that and hold that.

Captain: Well, we'll see what happens...

Jump seat Captain: We're going down now. I'll apply a little bit more power. I'm gonna try and set about ninety percent and see if that holds up good for you. Tryin' to find the right power setting so you don't have to fight this pitch.

First Officer: Ease it to the right.

Captain: Did you ever get hold of SAM?

Flight Engineer: Yep. Didn't get any help.

Captain: [Sound of laughter] Okay, did you tell 'm to advise dispatch of our situation and what we're doing?

Flight Engineer: Yes, he knows.

Captain: No more right turns, no more. Ah, I mean, ah, we want to turn right. He [Sioux City] wants us to turn right.

Jump seat Captain: You do want to turn...all right?

Captain: [Sound of exhalation]

First Officer: Where is Sioux City from our present position, United two thirty-two?

Sioux City Approach: United two thirty-two, it's about twenty on the heading and thirty-seven miles...

First Officer: There is an airport right below us here, but...

Captain: They say it won't accommodate us.

First Officer: Okay.

Captain: See if you can keep us with the throttles in a ten to fifteen-degree turn...

Jump seat Captain: All right. I'll play'em. I'll play 'em. I'll power up this number three engine and try to accommodate you.

Captain: You had the thing leveled off for a minute.

A United Airlines training pilot who had been riding in first class (Denny Fitch) comes into the cockpit to see whether he can assist the crew. The jump seat captain gives him his place, and he goes back into the cabin and takes a seat in the rear of the airplane. (I do not know this passenger's name. Therefore, I am unsure if he perished or not.)

Captain: My Name's Al Haynes.

Training Pilot: Hi, Al. Denny Fitch.

Captain: How do you do, Denny?

Training Pilot: I'll tell you what. We'll have a beer when this is all done.

Captain: Well, I don't drink, but I'll have one. Little right turns, little right turns.

The captain and his crew discuss power setting and headings for a few seconds.

Training Pilot: You lost the engine, huh?

Captain: Yeah, well, yeah. It blew. We couldn't do anything about it. We shut it down.

Training Pilot: Yeah.

Flight Engineer: Go ahead with any help you can give us.

Maintenance: United Two thirty-two, understand that you have one and three engines operating. You have absolutely no hydraulic power. You have no control over the aircraft. Is that correct?

Captain: Can't think of anything that we [haven't] done… There really isn't a procedure for this.

Training Pilot: No, the only thing I can think about that might help you at some point here [is to put] the landing gear down and that might hold the nose down a bit.

Maintenance: Okay, United two thirty-two, I've got operational engineering on its way over here, and at the present time you are doing just about everything that you can possibly do. Your flaps and slats, I believe, are in the up position, are they not?

Sioux City Approach: When you get turned to that two-forty heading, sir, the airport will be about twelve o'clock and thirty-eight miles.

First Officer: Okay, we're tryin' to control it just by power alone now. We have no hydraulics at all, so we're doing our best here.

Sioux City Approach: Roger, and we've notified the equipment out in that area, sir. The equipment is standing by.

Flight Engineer to Maintenance: That is affirmative. That is affirmative. That is affirmative. Do you read?

Captain Haynes confirms certain frequencies and heading for the final approach.

Captain: Everybody ready?

Training Pilot: Anything above about two ten [knots] is going to give you a nose-up moment...

Captain: We have almost no control of the airplane.

Maintenance: United two thirty-two, in your handbook on page 1 ninety-one, 1 ninety-one...

First Officer: We have no hydraulics at all.

Captain: It's gonna be tough, gonna be rough.

Flight Attendant: So, we're gonna evacuate?

Captain: Yeah. Well, we're gonna have the gear down.

Flight Attendant: Yeah.

Captain: And if we can keep the airplane on the ground and stop standing up, give us a second or two before you evacuate.

Flight Engineer: We already have a no flap-no slat made up and we're getting' ready. We're gonna try to put into Sioux City with gear down.

First Officer: Okay…pull back a little more.

Captain: 'Brace' will be the signal; it'll be over the PA system—'Brace, brace, brace'.

Maintenance: United, you're tryin' to go into Sioux City. We'll contact Sioux City and have emergency equipment available.

Flight Attendant: And that will be to evacuate?

Captain: No, that'll be to brace for landing.

Flight Attendant: Uh huh.

Captain: And then if you have to evacuate, you'll get the command signal to evacuate, but I really have my doubts you'll see us standing up, honey. Good luck, sweetheart.

Flight Attendant: Thank you. You too.

Flight Engineer: Okay, we will be tryin' to get in there.

Maintenance: Okay, United two thirty-two, I'll stay with you.

Flight Engineer: Okay, we will be waitin' in case you have anything more.

Maintenance: We're scurrying around, and I've got people out looking for more information.

Captain: The heading is two forty.

Training Pilot: Okay, I'm gonna try to hold you about two ten. I'll just see if it makes a difference if I bump it…bump it up in the air. This may be the world's greatest tricycle…

Flight Engineer: She says there appears to be some damage on that one wing. Do you want me to go back and take a look?

Training Pilot: No, we don't have time.

Captain: Okay, go ahead. Go ahead and see what you can see; not that it'll do any good.

Captain: I wish we had a little better control of the elevator. They told us the autopilot would do this, but it won't. Try yours again.

First Officer: Can't get it on.

Captain: Well, we've got the ah…ah.

Training Pilot: All right, we came into the clear.

Captain: Turn baby.

Training Pilot: Which way do you want it Al?

Captain: Left.

First Officer: Left.

Captain: Come on back, come on back, come on back…as soon as that [is] vertical go for it, go for it. Watch that vertical speed the second it starts to move. Come back, come back, come back. Go for it. If we can get this under control elevator-wise we can work on steer later.

Cockpit sound: [Sound of laughter]

Training Pilot: We need to go left again to get ready to go…

Captain: You keep goin' right two forty 'cause we still got two thousand feet to go.

Captain: United two thirty-two, we're gonna have to continue one more right turn. We got the elevators pretty much under control within three or four hundred feet but we still can't do much with the steering.

Sioux City Approach: United two thirty-two heavy, roger. Understand you [have] the elevators possibly under control [enough to hold] altitude?

First Officer: Barely.

Captain: Negative. We don't have it, but we are better, that's all.

Sioux City Approach: Roger.

Training Pilot: You want to turn right?

Captain: Yeah, let's turn right.

Training Pilot: All right, here we go.

Captain: How far is the field now, please?

Sioux City Approach: United two thirty-two heavy, you're currently thirty-three miles north-east.

Cockpit Sound: [Sound of three knocks on the door]

Captain: Thank you.

Captain: Just let her ease down. I wish they'd unlock that door, pull the circuit breaker on that door. Just unlock it, will ya?

Flight Engineer: Okay.

Sioux City Approach: United two thirty-two heavy, there are a couple of really small airports out in the vicinity here, and Storm Lake is four thousand two hundred feet by seventy-five. That's about fifteen miles east of your position.

Flight Engineer: All right, I walked to the back and we got a lot of damage to the tail section. We could see through the window.

First Officer: Roger, we're still goin' down tryin' to control it. As we get down a little lower here, we'll pick it out.

Maintenance: Okay, United two thirty-two, you have a lot of damage to the tail section?

Flight Engineer: The leading edge of the elevator is damaged. I mean, there's damage there that I can see. I don't know how much [there] is that I cannot see. I can see it on the leading edge, on the outer parts.

Maintenance: United two thirty-two, Engineering is assembling right now, and they're listening to us.

Captain Haynes announces his orders through the public address system about the warning to "brace."

Flight Engineer: Okay, number two engine blew. Severe shudders and vibration through the airplane when it blew. Then we tried to pull the throttle back on number two. It wouldn't come back. It was frozen. We shut it down, turned off the fuel in that, pulled the fire handle on it, and we have only been able to hold direction control through power application. We're down to nine thousand now and we're trying to make Sioux City. We're gonna have to use alternate gear to get the gear down. I think we're gonna be kinda busy here. If there's anything I can talk to you about, I'll try to. If there's anything you can give for suggestions, give me a holler.

Sioux City Approach: United two thirty-two heavy, there is a small airport at twelve o'clock and seven miles. The runway is four thousand feet long there.

First Officer: Hey, I'm controlling it myself now. As soon as the captain gets back on, he'll give me a hand here. He's talking on the PA.

Captain: Okay, let's start this sucker down a little more.

Jump seat Training Pilot: Okay, set your power a little bit.

Captain: Anybody have any ideas about [what to do about the landing gear]? He [the Engineer] is talking to SAM.

Jump seat Training Pilot: Yeah, he's talking to SAM. I'm gonna alternate gear. Maybe that will even help you. If there is no fluid, I don't know how the outboard ailerons are going to help you.

Captain: How do we get the gear down?

Jump seat Training Pilot: Well, they can freefall. The only thing is, we alternate the gear. We got the [landing gear] doors down?

Captain: Yep.

First Officer: We're gonna have trouble stopping too.

Captain: Oh, yeah. We don't have any brakes.

First Officer: No brakes?

Captain: Well, we have some brakes [but not much].

Jump seat Training Pilot: [Braking will be a] one-shot deal. Just mash it, mash it once. That's all you get. I'm gonna turn ya. [I'm gonna] give you a left turn back to the airport. Is that okay?

Captain: I got it. Okay, United two thirty-two, we're starting to turn back to the airport. Since we have no hydraulics, braking [it's] gonna really be a problem. Would suggest the equipment be toward the far end of the runway. I think under the circumstances, regardless of the condition of the airplane when we stop, we're going to evacuate. So, you might notify the ground crew that we're gonna do that.

Sioux City Approach: United two thirty-two heavy, wilco, sir. If you can continue that left turn to about two-twenty heading sir, that'll take you right to the airport.

First Officer: Two-twenty, roger.

Captain: What's your ceiling right now?

Jump seat Training Pilot: How far away are we from the airport? How far from the airport?

Sioux City Approach: Ah, ceiling is four thousand, broken, and visibility's one five underneath it.

Captain: And the airport elevation?

Sioux City Approach: One thousand ninety-eight.

First Officer: Well, five thousand feet we ought to break out. If you have any problem about the spoilers Al, we won't have those either, will we?

Captain: I don't think that'll help. I'm off for just a second to buckle up.

First Officer: All right.

Jump seat Training Pilot: You can tell me what you need. Holler what you need...

Captain: What did SAM say? Good luck?

Flight Engineer: He hasn't said anything.

Captain: Okay, well forget them. Tell 'em you're leaving the air, and you're gonna come back up here and help us... Ease her down just a little bit.

Jump seat Training Pilot: When you get a chance ask them how far out we are.

Captain: How far are we away from the airport now?

Sioux City Approach: Thirty-five miles, and if you continue that left turn about another fifteen or twenty degrees it'll take you right to the runway.

Captain: Okay. We don't have a localizer or a glide slope, so...

Sioux City Approach: Yes sir. You're well too far north of it now.

Captain: Okay.

Maintenance: United two thirty-two, one more time. No hydraulic quantity, is that correct?

Captain: Now we gotta level off a little bit. We're six thousand feet above the field right [now].

Unknown: Yeah, right.

Captain: About eighteen miles is where we want to be on the glide slope. We got about twelve miles to go before you want...

Flight Engineer: Affirmative, affirmative, affirmative.

Jump seat Training Pilot: Oh, yeah, we'll be with power.

Flight Engineer: Add a couple of knots for those speeds up there.

Jump seat Training Pilot: All right.

Captain: Anybody got any idea about puttin' the gear down right now?

Jump seat Training Pilot: All right, I would. I would suggest...

Captain: Should we free fall it?

First Officer: Yeah, yeah. I got to get out of the way to get the door.

Captain: Put it down.

For the next few seconds, the crew discusses the best way to get the landing gear down without hydraulic pressure. They will either use gravity and let the gear fall out, or they will crank it down manually.

Captain: Okay, put it down.

Jump seat Training Pilot: I don't know. I don't have any great ideas.

First Officer: Try it out.

Sioux City Approach: United two thirty-two heavy, your present heading looks good.

Captain: We'll see how close we can come to holding it.

First Officer: Apply a little power.

Jump seat Training Pilot: I can slow you down. Do you want to go one eighty-five?

Captain: Nope.

Flight Engineer: Green.

Captain: Go for it. Go ahead. Keep it at [one] eighty-five. Okay, start it down now. Ease back.

Flight Engineer: Gear handle down. Gear handle down.

Captain: Okay, lock up and put everything away.

Jump seat Training Pilot: There go the slats.

Captain: A little right turn. Don't have much to do. Sit down and lock up. Get up there and see what he is doin' for power.

Unknown: Here we go.

Unknown: I want to stay level if we can if we're not too far out.

Captain: Okay, right turns. Level up first. Or level up our turn. Straighten out the turn. Get yourself all buttoned up.

Cockpit sound: [Sound of a groan].

Captain: Level up here.

Sioux City Approach: United two thirty-two heavy, can you still make the slight right turns?

Captain: Yeah. Right turns are no problem, just left turns…

Sioux City Approach: Roger

Captain: Well, momma. We'll [make or miss] those baseball games after all.

First Officer: Are you in good and tight?

Jump seat Training Pilot: I'm not in at all, Bill.

First Officer: No, not you. But him...

Jump seat Training Pilot: Yeah. It seems [we're gonna have to keep more power on the right engine.

Sioux City Approach: United two thirty-two heavy, Sir, you are well too far north.

Captain: Pull it back.

Captain: We know.

Unknown: How many miles?

Sioux City Approach: Two thirty-two heavy, your present heading is a little close, Sir. Can you make a shallow left turn about ten degrees or so?

Captain: I'll try.

First Officer: Back on the controls.

Jump seat Training Pilot: Got to get my glasses on or I can't see.

First Officer: Where's the airport?

Sioux City Approach: United two thirty-two, the airport's currently twelve o'clock and two one miles.

Captain: Twenty-one miles and thousand feet. We got to level off.

Sioux City Approach: United two thirty-two heavy, you're gonna have to widen out just slightly to your left, Sir, to make the turn to final and also, it'll take you away from the city.

Captain: A little left bank.

Captain: Whatever you do, keep us away from the city.

Captain: Back, Back.

Jump seat Training Pilot: Hold this thing level if you can.

Captain: Level, baby, level, level…

Flight Engineer: We're turning now.

Jump seat Training Pilot: More power, more power, give 'em more power.

First Officer: More power, full power.

Jump seat Training Pilot: Power picks 'em up.

Sioux City Approach: United two thirty-two heavy, fly heading one eight zero, one eighty…

Captain: I don't think that we can do that, but we'll try.

Unknown: Right turn, throttle back.

Captain: Can we turn left?

Sioux City Approach: You are currently one seven miles north-east of the airport. You're doing good…

Captain: It has to be a right turn to one eighty. We can't do anything about it…

Flight Engineer: Do you want this seat?

Jump seat Training Pilot: Yes, do you mind?

Flight Engineer: I don't mind. I think that you know what you're doing there before.

Captain: Level it off.

Sioux City Approach: United two thirty-two heavy, there's a tower five miles off to your right side that's three thousand four hundred in height.

First Officer: Roger.

Jump seat Training Pilot: Keep turning right, Al. Keep turning right.

Captain: You got to level this sucker off. The only thing that I was afraid of was putting the gear down in case we have to ditch.

Sioux City Approach: United two thirty-two heavy, how steep a right turn can you make, Sir?

Unknown: Right.

Captain: We got to go one-eighty. Right is the only way to go. So, we can't control the airplane. That way… [Sound of laughter]

First Officer: All right, we're gonna have to try it straight ahead, Al. I think what we're gonna have to do…

Sioux City Approach: United two thirty-two heavy, if you can hold that altitude, Sir, the right turn to one-eighty would put you on about ten miles east of the airport.

Captain: That's what we're tryin' to do.

First Officer: Let's see if we can get a shallow descent, Al.

Captain: That's what I'm tryin' to do… Get this thing under control. When it starts up, push.

First Officer: Okay. Here we go. Push hard, push hard.

Jump seat Training Pilot: When the speed bleeds [creeps] back you'll catch it. Now, where do you want to go?

Captain: Want to keep turnin' right. Want to go to the airport.

Jump seat Training Pilot: You want to go to the airport.

Captain: About a thirty-degree bank.

Sioux City Approach: United two thirty-two heavy, roger. Turn right heading one eight zero.

First Officer: One eighty.

Captain: We got to level this sucker off. Come back, come back, come back.

Jump seat Training Pilot: I got the tower.

Captain: Come back, come back. All the way back.

Jump seat Training Pilot: I can't handle that steep a bank. Can't handle that steep a bank.

Sioux City Approach: United two thirty-two heavy, be advised there is a four-lane highway up in that area, Sir, if you can pick that up.

Captain: Okay, we'll see what we can do here. We've already put down the gear and we're gonna have to be puttin' [down] on something solid if we can...

Jump seat Training Pilot: Wish we hadn't put that gear down.

Flight Engineer: Ah, well.

Jump seat Training Pilot: We don't know.

Captain: Just keep turnin' if you can.

Jump seat Training Pilot:
Which way do you want to go?

Captain: I want to get as close to the airport as we can.

Jump seat Training Pilot: Okay.

Captain: If we have to set this thing down in dirt, we set it in the dirt.

Unknown: Speed's too low; watch the angle.

Captain: Get on the air and tell them we got about four minutes to go.

First Officer: We've got about three or four minutes to go, [it] looks like.

Captain: PA system, PA system... Tell the passengers [to brace].

Flight Engineer: We have four minutes to touchdown, four minutes to touchdown...

Sioux City Approach: United two thirty-two heavy, roger. Can you pick up a road or something up there?

First Officer: We're tryin' it. Still anywhere from two thousand up to fifteen hundred feet, down now, in waves.

Jump seat Training Pilot: Which way do you want to go?

Captain: Right, right, right. We gotta go...

Unknow: Speed up!

Jump seat Training Pilot: Airport's down there. Got it.

Captain: I don't see it yet.

First Officer: Soon as it starts down, back we go...

Unknown: Not too much back...

First Officer: Okay, now you can bring 'em up.

Unknown: Keep turning, keep turning, keep turning.

First Officer: There's the airport.

Sioux City Approach: United two thirty-two heavy, the airport is about eighteen miles south-east of your position, about two-twenty on the heading, but we're gonna need you southbound away from the city first. If you can hold one-eighty heading...

First Officer: We're tryin', tryin' to get to it right now.

Jump seat Training Pilot: If I keep you about two hundred knots, I seem to be able to get enough control...

Sioux City Approach: United two thirty-two heavy, advise if you can pick up a road or anything where you can possibly land it on that.

Captain: Okay, we're a hundred eighty-degree heading. Now what do you want?

Sioux City Approach: United two thirty-two, if you can hold the altitude, the one-eighty heading will work fine for about seven miles.

Captain: Okay, we're tryin' to turn back.

Captain: Forward, make a left turn, left...

Jump seat Training Pilot: No left at all.

Captain: No left at all?

Jump seat Training Pilot: I'll give you some.

First Officer: Okay, now it's...

Captain: Back, back, back, back...forward, forward, forward. Won't this be a fun landing? Back [sound of laughter].

Sioux City Approach: United two thirty-two heavy, can you hold that heading, Sir?

First Officer: Yeah, we're on it now for a little while.

Sioux City Approach: United two thirty-two heavy roger. That heading will put your currently fifteen miles north-east of the airport. If you can hold that, it'll put you on about a three-mile final.

First Officer: Okay, we're givin' it heck.

Captain: I'll tell you what. I'll write off your PC [Pilot Certificate} if we make this...when we make this. Hold the heading if you can... That's fine. Turn left. Help me turn left so we know what it's doing. Back, back, back.

Sioux City Approach: United two thirty-two heavy, the airport's currently twelve o'clock and one three miles.

First Officer: Okay, we're lookin' for it.

Captain: Forward, forward, forward.

First Officer: Twelve o'clock at thirteen miles. We have to start down, but...

Jump seat Training Pilot: Ask what the field elevation is.

Captain: Field elevation is what again?

First Officer: A thousand eighty.

Sioux City Approach: Ah, eleven hundred feet, one thousand one hundred...

Captain: Okay, thank you.

Jump seat Training Pilot: Let's start down. We have to ease it down.

Captain: We're startin' down a little bit now. We got a little better control of the elevator.

Sioux City Approach: United two thirty-two heavy, roger. The airport's currently at your one o'clock position, one zero miles.

Captain: Ease it down, ease it down...

Cockpit sound: [Sound of groan, sound of exhalation].

Jump seat Training Pilot: I got the runway if you don't...

Captain: I don't... Come back, come back.

Jump seat Training Pilot: It's off to the right over there.

First Officer: Right there. Let's see if we can hold five hundred feet a minute.

Sioux City Approach: United two thirty-two heavy, if you can't make the airport, sir, there is an interstate that runs north to south, to the east side of the airport. It's a four-lane interstate.

Jump seat Training Pilot: See? We got tower [in sight] right here at our one o'clock low...

Captain: We're just passing it right now. We're gonna try for the airport.

Captain: Is that the runway right there?

Unknown: Right.

Captain: We have the runway in sight. We have the runway in sight. We have the runway in sight. We'll be with you shortly. Thanks a lot for your help.

Jump seat Training Pilot: Bring it on down... Ease 'er down.

First Officer: Oh, baby.

Jump seat Training Pilot: Ease her down.

Captain: Tell 'em that we're just two minutes from landing.

Sioux City Approach: United two thirty-two heavy, the wind's currently three six zero at one one three sixty at eleven. You're cleared to land on any runway...

Captain: [Laughter]. Roger. [Laughter] You want to be particular and make it a runway, huh?

Flight Engineer (on PA): Two minutes.

This is when Captain Haynes announces to "Brace, brace, brace." In the passenger cabin, the attendants begin shouting for passengers to get their heads down. The first flight attendant yells commands.

Jump seat Training Pilot: What's the wind?

Captain: Say the wind one more time.

Sioux City Approach: Wind's zero one, zero at one one...

First Officer: Yeah, we want to go down.

Jump seat Training Officer: Yeah, I can see the runway, but I got to keep control on ya.

First Officer: Pull it off a little.

Captain: See if you can get us a left turn.

First Officer: Left turn, just a hair Al.

Captain: Okay, we're all three talking at once. Say it again one more time.

Sioux City Approach: Zero one, zero at one one, and there is a runway that's closed, sir, that could probably work to the south. It runs north-east to southwest.

Captain: We're pretty well lined up on this one here…

Jump seat Training Pilot: I'll pull the spoilers on the touch.

Captain: Get the brakes on with me.

Sioux City Approach: United two thirty-two heavy, roger, sir. That's a closed runway, sir, that'll work, sir. We're getting' the equipment off the runway. They'll line up for that one.

Captain: How long is it?

Sioux City Approach: Sixty-six hundred feet, six thousand six hundred. Equipment's comin' off.

Captain: Pull the power back. That's right. Pull the left one back.

First Officer: Pull the left one back.

Sioux City Approach: At the end of the runway it's just wide-open field.

Unknown: Left throttle, left, left, left, left…

Unknown: God!

Cockpit sound: [Sound of impact]

End of tape.

28

A Victim's Final Resting Place

Twenty-one years after the most devastating, life-altering day of my life, my parents were on a casual road trip near Tin Cup and St. Elmo, Colorado. Known throughout history as a prominent mining town, it is now a ghost town of a few summer homes, with only a small number of year-round residents. Tourists, including myself, like to visit and step back into another time.

My parents presented me with a couple of pictures that they took on July 19, 2010, while they were visiting this historical town. They said that the date of death on a certain tombstone caught their attention. Following is a copy of the photos that they took.

I was taken back by the date of death, July 19, 1989, and the fact that they were at the cemetery on that exact date twenty-one years later. What were the odds of a victim of Flight 232 being buried in a small, lonely ghost town, ten thousand feet high in the Rocky Mountains? It seemed like a long shot, but I had to know if Vada Smith was on Flight 232. I was not familiar with all of the victim's names, but after some research, I discovered that, yes, Vada was on our fateful flight and was one of those who perished. She had been seated in first class, seat 01B.

Vada Ann Carey Smith, a wife, mother, and sister, was only five months from her forty-first birthday when she died. I do not know anything about Vada's life, the cause of her injuries which accounted for her death, or why she was flying to either Chicago or onward to Philadelphia. However, thirty-two years later, her life and death still have an effect on me. What kind of person was she? How many children did she leave behind? What was her occupation? What were her thoughts after the explosion when the plane was bucking and shuddering as the pilots were trying to control and land it? Why did her family decide to bury her in Iron City Cemetery?

I ask these questions and more as I think of the 112 passengers who didn't survive Flight 232. In the current age of the Internet, there is a lot of information online about the crash of Flight 232, but still many questions and no answers about those who perished. All of us that were seated when that flight took off were connected during those forty minutes, but afterward, just like the pieces and parts of the aircraft, we ended up scattered and disconnected. For those of us who survived, our lives were in pieces and permanently altered. Of course, a few of us have stayed minimally connected through the years, and may think of one another now and then, and contact a fellow passenger we feel close to, but our memories and stories are still all so different.

29

A Book, a Death, and a New Beginning

In 2012, some of the survivors and myself were interviewed by Laurence Gonzales, author of *Flight 232, A Story of Disaster and Survival.* He interviewed me on March 17 and May 20, 2012. At this time, my then-husband Tim and I still lived in Page, Arizona. I remember being skeptical, hesitant, and nervous about being interviewed by an author, especially someone I had never met. Mr. Gonzales scheduled the interviews for specific times and dates to accompany my schedule, so I had plenty of time to think and gather my memories to tell him my story. During each of his calls, I chose to sit outside on the porch of our house which faced east, in Greenhaven, a small town ten miles outside of Page, in which I had a very clear and remarkable view of Navajo Mountain, as well as an unobstructed view of the very back of Wahweap Bay on Lake Powell. Not being sure of what kind of questions I would be asked, I just let my mind and memories open up while I was on the phone talking to Mr. Gonzales. I knew that he would be taking me on a trip back to July 19, 1989, and I needed a clear head. Mr. Gonzales was very professional, as well as attentive and caring as I related my story of Flight 232 during his interviews with me.

In late December of 2012, I received a rough draft of his book. At the time, he had titled it "Hard Alpha, The Crash of United Flight 232." He wanted each of the survivors that he interviewed for the book to read it and comment on, make any corrections, or suggestions as it pertained to ourselves. It was very surreal sitting down and reading this draft. Not also was my story in it, but the stories of some of my fellow friends and survivors. We all had a different perspective and, of course, different recollections and stories to tell. Many different paths and directions evolved from one major incident. Personally, I lived the crash all over again. By this time, I had forgotten how many times I had relived it.

During the next two years before the book was published, changes were made by myself and by the others who were interviewed, as well as the title of the book. Finally, we were told that the book would be published and available during the twenty-fifth anniversary, July 19, 2014.

Tim and I relocated to Colorado in July of 2012. We moved back to be closer to our children (my son Bryson and daughter Molly, as well as his two daughters, Sarah and Jenny). Even though Tim worked from home and had been with a great company as a project manager for about the last twelve years, we also decided that job opportunities in Denver would be better for both of us if anything happened. Sometimes his health was poor, and he decided not to travel for the company anymore. That also meant that there could be changes to his job in the future.

After a long drive back, with the moving van a few hours ahead of us we took our time, as we weren't meeting up with the moving van for a couple of days. We had already secured a house in Pueblo, with Nick (my son-in-law) and Molly's help that we would be renting for a while until we could decide where we really wanted to live. After leaving my wonderful job in accounts payable that I held at a multimillion-dollar resort just over the Arizona/Utah border, I was concerned that I could not secure a job in Pueblo. I sent out resumes and applied online for various employment opportunities, but nothing was offered in my line of work. It was a hard time economically to find a job. Tim became stressful with the situation of his job also. He kept telling me that I wasn't looking hard enough for a job. I was, so, of course, that brought on more disagreements and stress between the two of us.

After about two months, I did land a cashier job but was hoping to stay with it for only about a year until we could move closer to Denver. During that year, our marriage went sour, and Tim's job started to decline. I worked some horrible ours (2:30 a.m. to 11:00 a.m.), and when I would come home from work around eleven-thirty, Tim would be sitting in front of the television with his laptop appearing to work but wasn't. We had a nice office desk upstairs that he used to work from, but he told me that his company didn't have much for him to do from home lately. By this time, a year after we had moved back, I was becoming very frustrated and resentful toward Tim and our situation. I began looking for a small studio apartment in which to live and asked him for a divorce.

I never did move into that apartment or get a divorce. I came home from work one day and found him deceased in the truck inside the closed garage. That day is still very vivid in my memory. When I tried to open the garage to park the car inside, I realized the remote opener would not work. I tried to manually open it, but it would not budge. It was then that I heard a low rumble. At first, I thought it was the air conditioner running since it was a warm day in June, but it wasn't. As I let myself through the front door, I immediately opened the door to my right that opened onto the garage.

The garage was full of exhaust from the running truck inside and in the driver seat, slumped over to the right was Tim. After I opened the truck door, I tried to wake him by shaking him, but he was unresponsive. By this time, I was hysterical but was able to reach across his still body and turn off the truck. I found my wits just long enough to dial 911. That was my second 911 call I had to make in my life. (The first one was shortly after the crash when I was married to my first husband, Ron.)

Before the paramedics arrived, I found a note on the kitchen counter with Tim's wedding ring placed on top of it. He had written: "You bought it, you keep it." He was referring to me having to buy our wedding rings from some of my airline settlement because at the time we wanted to marry, he had been ill and out of work for a while.

He always said that he would pay me back, and he did in various ways through the twenty-one years we were married.

Soon after my 911 call, the paramedics with a fire truck arrived, as well as the police and an advocate for these types of situations. While the emergency team proceeded with their work, checking me, my dog, the house and garage for carbon monoxide levels, the advocate sat with me to try to calm me down. I was able to give her the name of my daughter and Molly's employment so that she could be contacted. I also called my parents in Littleton. My mother answered, but she could not understand what I was saying and asked who I was. My throat was closing up on me from the hysteria, so the advocate had to take over the phone call and explain the situation. After their conversation, I was told that my parents were on their way. They did not hesitate to make the two-hour drive from Littleton to Pueblo.

In the meantime, Molly was on her way over, straight from work. I could not locate my son. I could not wait to have my family by my side. When Molly arrived, I fell into her arms, and we both hugged and cried until we were spent. It was a shock to her also. She and Nick knew that there were some problems with Tim and I, but couldn't believe that something like this would happen. When my parents arrived in the late afternoon, the emergency team had already left and took Tim's body away. My sister and niece came with my parents for my moral and emotional support also. My son-in-law Nick arrived soon after. I had most of my family there but still wanted my son there also.

My father, being the retired chief of police of Littleton and one of the people I depend and lean on, took control after asking me if I wanted him to. I remember I kept saying "I don't know what to do! I don't know what to do!"

He asked, "Do you want me to take control?"

"Yes!" I answered, not knowing which way to turn.

My life was once again on a downward spiral, but instead of being frightened inside an aircraft that was out of control, I was frightened and frantic in my own home. My father was like Captain Haynes and the rest of his crew. He took control, used his head, and worked things through, hoping for the best outcome. He immediately contacted his lawyer and explained the situation. I was to talk to "John" the next day, in which we would then proceed with everything that would be necessary. I had a long road ahead of me, and I had no idea which way that road would lead me in the days and months to come.

By now, I had been functioning on the few hours' sleep that I had gotten before I got up to go to work that morning. After locating Bryson, Molly and I went to pick him up and bring him to the house. After we returned home with Bryson, and making sure I was all right, my parents decided to leave to stay at a motel close by. Molly and Nick also decided to return home. Bryson, my sister Babette, and niece Katie, stayed the night with me. Sleep was hard in coming, but I finally fell asleep for a few hours before the sun rose on another summer day. I was now a widow. Something I never thought I would be.

The next day, my family returned to the house for more moral support, and we were able to make some plans and move forward with important actions that had to be accomplished. My lawyer, John, had instructed my father and I to proceed with a few sensitive legal matters. These included going to the county coroner's office so that I could release Tim's body after the autopsy so that he could be transported to Drinkwine Mortuary in Littleton, where he was to be cremated. Then we went to the bank and changed the accounts from joint to single accounts in my name. This was to protect the so-called "estate" of Tim and me. After returning home from another exhausting and emotional day, I found my dog Moki lying on the rug in front of the door that led to the garage. She lay there day and night knowing that was where Tim had been. After taking care of some more legal issues, my parents and the rest of my family left that afternoon to return home, and I found myself alone. I needed some time to process the situation, plus I preferred to be alone at that time. That night, as I lay in bed, thousands of thoughts and scenarios were running through my mind. I finally drifted off to sleep sometime in the predawn hours, only to be awakened by a caress on my left cheek. I sat straight up and was wide awake with the feeling that somebody was present in the bedroom. This may sound crazy, but I did feel Tim's presence in the room.

I said, "Go away, Tim. I'm fine." I was feeling very vulnerable, but I was still angry with him for what he had done. I finally got back to sleep afterward for a few hours. The next morning, I noticed that Moki was not lying on the rug by the door to the garage anymore.

I could not have the truck that I found Tim in anywhere around me where I could see it. Thankfully, my son-in-law Nick agreed to drive it and park it out front of their house. I know it was an emotional thing for him to do—to get behind that wheel and sit in that seat where Tim died a few days earlier, but he did it. I am forever grateful to him and Molly for their love and support. My lawyer John knew a person who would buy it from me (it was paid in full) and drive it away. It was a great relief to hand the title over to this person and watch him drive the truck away. I wouldn't ever see it again. This was one of the many things that I had to get rid of in order to move on with my life. Another thing was to sell the boat that Tim and I had for twenty years. There were many good memories and trips on Lake Powell with the family that included the boat. I was able to sell it to a good friend of mine who lived in Pueblo. Also, we were renting the house in Pueblo at the time of Tim's death so that was not a problem. I didn't have to go through the process of selling it.

Through the rest of the month after Tim died, I was busy dealing with his funeral, legal matters, and packing up the house. All the while, I am on a roller coaster ride with my emotions and relationships with Tim's family. Even though it was never admitted outright, I knew that some of his family blamed me for his death. It was shown by their actions before, during, and after his memorial. I was given the cold shoulder. No one in his family but one brother would talk to me. That brother was helpful with the cremation of Tim's body and did communicate with me.

Sadly, just days after Tim died, his older sister suddenly died. His whole family was reeling with both deaths. Out of respect, I went to her memorial but was treated with the same cold shoulder as I was at Tim's memorial. It was obvious that I was not welcome in their family anymore. To tell you the truth, I was hurt by their behavior, but I also had many obstacles and things to process in order to get my life back together and move on. I had to move forward, with or without their blessings. I also lost many things that were dear to me during this transition, as I had to downsize and get rid of a lot of personal items. To this day, I have not seen or spoken to any of Tim's family.

Three weeks after Tim's death, I moved from Pueblo to Colorado Springs into the unknown. I did have my immediate family supporting me with their love and encouragement. Eventually, I was able to start a new life and move on. One door closed, but another one opened yet again in my life. I met a wonderful man and remarried.

Kelly, my new husband was a pilot. He had been flying since his early twenties, in which he flew for forty-four years and had over five thousand hours flying when he was forced to retire due to medical reasons about four years after we were married. He started his military career in the Air Force and is a Vietnam veteran. After Vietnam, he joined the army and, after twenty-four years, retired as an Army lieutenant colonel. With his connections to the Air Force, we were married in the Air Force Academy Chapel in a very private ceremony with only my parents as witnesses and the Air Force chaplain. Being in the aviation industry as a flight engineer, pilot, and instructor pilot, he was able to relate to my history with the airplane crash. He had witnessed one of Captain Haynes's seminars regarding Flight 232. It had been a large part of his training.

Kelly stated in reference to those of us on Flight 232: "You were introduced to God on your way up (while in the air) and got acquainted with God on your way down." (I know that a lot of praying was going on all throughout the aircraft.)

The glider pilot instructing me. She did most of the flying from the rear seat while we were in the air but did let me take the controls for a little while.

In February 2015, Kelly gave me a gift for a glider flight as a Valentine present. I enjoyed watching the gliders at the Air Force Academy airport fly and circle around when I went to the airport with him. There was something so very serene and calming as I would watch a glider being towed behind an aircraft and then watching it float in the air after it was released. My thoughts and feelings were light and carefree as if I were in heaven when I watched the gliders. Kelly made it possible for me to actually have that experience. It was amazing! Nothing like being in a crippled DC-10 thirty-seven thousand feet in the air. I wished Flight 232 could have been like this glider ride. We would have floated down to earth with no problems.

One of my first flights with Kelly, my private pilot.

*Confident that I was going to "take the aircraft"
later. It was a wonderful flight.*

Pilot Kelly

Kelly told me some amazing stories, had some close calls, and some emergency situations from his life as a pilot. While in the Air Force, he was a C-130 flight engineer and an Air Force crew chief on a F-100, F-4, A-37, and T-37 aircraft. He held many airline ratings which are:

- ❖ Airline transport pilot rating; multi-engine
- ❖ CES500 type rating (corporate jet)
- ❖ Commercial pilot with instrument rating for single engine
- ❖ Airframe and powerplant license with an inspection authorization
- ❖ Flight instructor gold seal, with basic advanced and instrument flight instructor certificates
- ❖ Chief of academics of the US Air Force flight screening program through a government contractor: DOS Aviation.

Being a pilot, mechanic, and instructor, he taught all of these to other potential pilots through his years of aviation. The Lord knows that I felt safe, confident, and comfortable during the flights he and I took together. I'm sure we all pray that the pilot who has our lives in their hands whenever we board on any type of airplane is this seasoned and experienced. My husband and Captain Haynes were both pros during their aviation careers. I have nothing but heartfelt respect, admiration, and love for both of them.

30

Twenty-Fifth Anniversary of Flight 232

When the twenty-fifth anniversary was approaching, I was excited and apprehensive at the same time.

The trip to Sioux City was extremely important to me, and I was blessed to have my husband Kelly, daughter Molly, and son-in-law Nick with me. I hadn't made this journey to Sioux City since the first year anniversary when I went with my father. The ten-hour, 650-mile drive to Sioux City, Iowa, was long but very much worth it for the twenty-fifth-year anniversary of the crash.

After arriving in Sioux City and checking into our hotel, we decided to go to the Flight 232 Memorial, which is located along the bank of the Missouri River in Chris Larsen Park. There is a large sign just outside the park that states that you are in the right place to view the memorial.

I'm back in Sioux City, where my life changed twenty-five years ago.

"There are certain moments in life you simply have to enter."
(This is my favorite quote on one of the large stones
on the path leading to the memorial.)

While we were standing in front of the memorial, I noticed two people coming toward us. My first thought was that it was someone coming to also view the memorial before the full day of the remembrance started the next day. As they got closer, I realized it was my dear friend and fellow survivor Garry Priest and a friend of his. It was surreal. The Lord's timing is so perfect. Even though Garry had been a stranger twenty-five years ago, the Lord still put us in each other's path before, during, and after the crash. And now, on the twenty-fifth anniversary, he placed us in each other's path again.

I hadn't seen Garry since Captain Haynes was in Colorado Springs in October 1999 when we were both there for one of his many speeches that he gave across the country since his retirement in 1991. My daughter Molly was also glad to see Garry. She hadn't seen him in twenty years. But now she was a grown married woman, and Garry was also surprised and happy to see her. After hugs of hello and introductions all around, we all stood by the memorial and got caught up on each other's lives. Not knowing if we would run into each other again in the next few days, we took pictures to remember and mark this special time in our lives.

The following two pictures were taken in front of the 232-memorial statue of myself and Garry Priest, and myself and my husband Kelly.

*From left to right are my son-in-law Nick, my
daughter Molly, myself, and Kelly.*

As it turned out, Garry's and my paths did not cross anymore
during the three days we were in Sioux City for the remembrance
activities. However, I was very blessed to see him when I did, and

throughout the remembrance activities, I saw some other survivors and very dear friends of mine.

On the evening of July 18, 2014, at 7:00 p.m., there was a gathering at the Sioux City Orpheum Theatre: What Happened, What We've Learned and What Has Changed. This was a program to honor responders, families and recognize new volunteer efforts. It was led by Jim Wharton with United Airlines Captain Haynes, Jan Brown, Bob Hamilton, Gary Brown, Sr. Margaret Wick. Col. Dennis Swanstrom, Dr. David Greco, and Dr. Larry Foster.

Earlier that evening, outside the Orpheum Theatre, I ran into Captain Haynes. I identified myself, and he was gracious to comply when I asked to have a picture taken with him. Upon entering the theater, I noticed there were a lot of people milling around, taking pictures, and waiting for the program to begin. I ran into my fellow rescuer and seatmate, Rod Vetter. There wasn't that much time to get caught up with him then, as the program was about to begin. However, we agreed to meet each other at a certain restaurant the next evening in order to get caught up.

During the hour-and-one-half program, there was a lot of recaps of the crash and the actions of the responders. Many of the "heroes" were recognized and introduced. Some of them were in the audience, including Sioux City approach controller Kevin Bauchman and KTIV Channel 4 News camera operator Dave Boxum. This was the first time I had ever seen these two men. Kevin was the calm, cool, and collected voice in the Sioux City control tower that Captain Haynes communicated with during the forty minutes he was trying to control the aircraft. Dave was the camera operator whose famous footage of the aircraft crashing, taken behind a fence, was seen worldwide that same day and is still viewed numerous times on the Internet, even to this day. Lt. Colonel Dennis Nielsen, who is the subject of the memorial, carrying three-year-old Spencer Bailey in his arms, was also recognized. Being among these heroes and fellow survivors twenty-five years later was emotional for everybody. I could hear some people sobbing as they were taken back all those years earlier as they relived their stories and emotions. There had been a lot of change during the past twenty-five years. Some people had retired, had a change of career, remarried, relocated, or died. Everybody involved that fateful day processed things differently and made different choices as to the rest of their lives. However, all it took was a gathering of remembrance to draw those people together again.

Captain Haynes and myself before the gathering at the Orpheum Theatre, July 18, 2014.

After driving all day earlier and the emotional toll of the afternoon and evening, my husband, daughter, son-in-law, and myself were ready to try and get a good night's sleep. We retired to our hotel rooms, looking forward to the next day, which was the actual anniversary date of the crash. I needed to be emotionally ready for it.

Saturday morning, July 19, 2014, arrived with the sun shining and a little haze, as is common in the Midwest. There was a lot to look forward to. The town of Sioux City had rolled out the red carpet for those of us visiting from out of town and the public that wanted to visit and be a part of the remembrance. There were various open houses and tours going on throughout the day from 9:00 a.m. to 12:00 noon. Later that afternoon at precisely 4:00 p.m., at the time the plane crashed twenty-five years earlier, there would be a wreath laying and benediction in the new Outdoor Garden.

Of course, I wanted to attend all of the open houses, so after a quick breakfast at the hotel, we went to Briar Cliff College first. Twenty-five years had changed the campus a lot from what I remembered, but as I walked around with my family, we came across the dorm room where I spent the longest night of my life. Even though I only slept a couple of hours that night, this was the room where my eyes closed on the worst day of my life and opened up the next day to a different life. An unknown but new life and future.

Captain Haynes and most of his flight crew.

While at Briar Cliff, in front of the *meis* Recital Hall, a group picture of some of the survivors and flight crew was taken. As I reflect on that picture now, I didn't realize how many of us had been there at the same time during that open house. Yet, again, some of us were brought together.

More survivors and the flight crew.

Author Laurence Gonzales and myself.

After leaving Briar Cliff, we went to The Security Institute, where author Laurence Gonzales would be signing his book *Flight 232, A Story of Disaster and Survival.* I was so anxious to finally meet him and obtain some copies of the book to give to my family and close friends. There were many people hovering around him and the table that was stacked with copies of his book. After introducing myself, I sat down and had him autograph all ten books that I purchased. It was so exciting to meet a real author and have my picture taken with him, all the time knowing that my story was in the very book that I was holding in my hands! He personally autographed one copy dedicated specifically to me. I will keep this copy with all of my other treasured memories of Flight 232. He again thanked me for being willing to share my story, and I thanked him for authoring the book.

The next place we visited during the open houses was the mobile van that was taking blood donations. The Life Serve Blood Center and the Mayor's Youth Commission was collecting blood to help reach a goal of collecting 232 units by the end of the weekend. I donated blood many times before, and of course, I was going to donate for this cause also. My daughter Molly and I took a few minutes to relax and donate our blood. I have shared a lot of such memories with Molly, and this was one more that we would remember in the years to come. Not just the donation of blood, which was always in high demand, but why we were there and what we were celebrating: my survival and just how precious life is. Who would think that by donating blood, one would truly be celebrating their own life, as well as knowing that they were helping others survive also, whatever the life-threatening situation may be? While lying there waiting for the units to fill, I kept thinking that twenty-five years ago, I could very well have been one of the people who had been critically injured and needed blood in order to survive. It gave me a very humbling feeling.

After a quick break for lunch, we wanted to go to the Mid America Museum of Aviation and Transportation to see the 232 exhibit. We were also anticipating the upcoming hour of 4:00 p.m. in which there would be a special remembrance ceremony for all those involved in Flight 232. The museum opened in 2010 on fifteen acres with thirty thousand square feet of display and exhibit space. The museum is located on runway 22, the old WWII closed runway that Captain Haynes and his crew were able to maneuver to in hopes of landing the crippled aircraft. There, in a large hangar, the nose, including the cockpit, of a United DC-10 aircraft was housed as part of the exhibit. Captain Alfred C. Haynes was stenciled on the outside. There was also a new Flight 232 Exhibit and Reflection Garden that had been dedicated as well just outside the museum. One-hundred-twelve evergreen trees have been planted as part of the garden—one tree for each passenger who died.

As we were driving to the museum, I realized that one of the streets we were on in the surrounding area was named Al Haynes Dr.

Captain Haynes reflecting.

Part of the United 232 display in the Mid-America Museum.

During our self-guided tour of the museum, I saw many items on display that took me back twenty-five years ago. As you first entered the exhibit, the above sign is posted. There is also a collage of photos of the emergency management drill that took place in 1987, two years prior to the 232 crash of a major airline disaster. One whole wall featured a picture of cornstalks in the cornfield and each victim's name listed on it. There was the timeline and flight path of 232 enlarged, which enabled it to be read, and various pictures of parts of the torn apart aircraft and the crash site. There were also a couple of the original seats that were on the aircraft and the seat that Captain Haynes sat in. Right next to that were mannequins wearing first responder turnout gear, the fireman's gear, and the 185th's captain suit. Some display cases held various pieces from the plane and other memorabilia, such as one of the passenger's boarding ticket. In a separate glass frame, the blouse that airline attendant Susan White wore was encased, showing the original dirt and soot on it. There was so much to look at. I am sure that if I were to go to the museum today, there would be even more parts of the exhibit that would have been added that are just as intriguing and memorable.

Before the four o'clock hour, there was a gathering inside the museum, in which a stage and a couple hundred of chairs had been set up. Two very iconic guest speakers were present: Captain Alfred C. Haynes and Jerry Schemmel. They both gave memorable speeches, although Captain Haynes's was noticeably short. He just wanted to thank everyone for being there and putting this remembrance together. The chilling rollcall of the names of the 112 who died was then read. Standing next to a large silver bell was a man wearing the dress uniform of a firefighter, including fire hat and white gloves. He rang the bell after each victim's name was read. There were a lot of tears as there were many people gathered in the audience who lost a loved one in the crash or were just remembering how much it had affected them, whether they were a survivor or part of the rescue efforts.

Afterward, some of the crew were available to tell the story of their experience. Three of the airline attendants sat down before the cameras, including senior flight attendant, Jan Brown, and flight attendant Susan White. For years, Jan Brown has lobbied Congress and the FAA to ensure safety for "lap children" on all airline flights. The FAA has never mandated the use of child restraint belts on an aircraft. This has been an ongoing lobby for years.

February 12, 2019, The Points Guys: On this year's "most wanted" list, the National Transportation Safety Board (NTSB) has released a number of its *most wanted transportation-related safety improvements.* On that list is the recommendation that the FAA disallow lap infants who can currently ride (*often for free) in parents' laps* until they turn two years old. The NTSB states that "children are safest when they are properly secured in a child safety seat, in their own seat, when flying" and would like the FAA to remove the exemption that permits babies and young children to fly as lap infants.

All of those in attendance left the hangar and walked outside to gather in the "Reflection Garden." There was a permanent marker at the sight where the right wing of the aircraft first made impact. A beautiful red, white, and blue wreath was displayed on that exact spot as many people gathered around to pause in a silent prayer for the victims who perished and to remember all of those involved with the crash. A bagpipe piper played a beautiful rendition of "Amazing Grace" after the moment of silence. Afterward, I was able to share a photo with Captain Haynes and Jerry Schemmel. They were two of the many heroes who changed so many lives the day that forced those involved to reexamine their lives going forward.

Standing with Captain Haynes at the spot where the plane first hit the ground twenty-five years ago. It is a permanent memorial.

Standing with my dear friend Jerry Schemmel

Later that evening, some of the survivors and their families met for dinner. I saw Rod Vetter again and Ron Sheldon. Ron had been seated in seat 19E, and Rod had been seated in seat 19D.

The three of us had this iconic picture taken twenty-five years after the crash.

Each of these gatherings was special, as we could not be sure if we would see each other throughout the rest of the remembrance. The next day was Sunday, July 20. A Sunday morning ecumenical service was planned to be held at the Anderson Dance Pavilion from 11:00 a.m.–12:00 noon.

Sunday morning was a beautiful day, with the blue skies of Iowa and the sun shining down on us. Since the whole remembrance weekend was open to the public, there were many people from the area that turned out for the Sunday service, in addition to those of us who had traveled from different parts of the United States to be there. It was a large gathering in which there was standing-room only under the pavilion, as all of the seats were filled. The service was led by Pastor Darrin Vick from Morningside Lutheran Church. The sermon was given by Rev. Greg Clapper, retired 185th ANG Chaplain. He was the reverend that was on sight the day of the crash. In conclusion to the service, there were readings by Father Marvin

Boes. Again, there were many tearful eyes throughout the gathering. The service concluded at the Spirit of Siouxland, the 232 Memorial which was next to the Anderson Dance Pavilion. The artist who created the life-size bronze sculpture of three-year-old Spencer Bailey and Lt. Col. Dennis Nielsen of the Iowa Air National Guard's 185th Tactical Fighter Group, Dale Lamphere would be present.

Dale Lamphere is a renowned artist from South Dakota, known for his full spectrum from classic figurative sculpture in cast bronze, to monumental fabricated stainless-steel sculpture involving design, fabrication, and structural engineering disciplines. He has created sixty major public sculptures. Personally, I think he did the city of Sioux City and all involved in Flight 232 a great honor in portraying the memory and the heroism of that day in history.

There were volunteers handing out red, white, and blue carnations for those present at the memorial. Some people laid their carnation in the arms of little Spencer Bailey on the sculpture. Others, like myself, kept theirs as a memento of the twenty-fifth-anniversary memorial. My dried blue carnation lies inside my copy of *Flight 232, A Story of Disaster and Survival.*

As the morning was winding down and people were getting ready to leave, I was able to meet up with Senior Flight Attendant, Jan Brown. She also honored me with a picture that I have added to my memories.

Jan Brown and myself after Sunday Memorial Service.

Some of us would not see each other again until the thirtieth anniversary.

31

Retirement

Captain Haynes retired on August 26, 1991 from United Airlines. He was just a couple of days shy of his sixtieth birthday. Sixty years of age was the mandatory retirement age for commercial airline pilots at that time. Since then, The Fair Treatment for Experienced Pilots Act (Public Law 110-135) went into effect on December 13, 2007, raising the age of retirement to age sixty-five.

After verifying the information with fellow survivor and airline attendant, Susan White, she told me that his last commercial flight with United Airlines was August 26, 1991 from Denver to Seattle. Peter Allen worked the flight as the engineer where Dudley sat. All the flight attendants from 232 worked the flight, and they put a rose in Rene Le Beau's jump seat and went understaffed, as they did not want anyone else working in her place. Garry Priest was at the press conference before the flight. Three Sioux City emergency workers were on the flight: Gary Brown, Jim Hathaway, and Dave Kaplan.

I am sorry that I wasn't a passenger on his last flight. It would have been another historical chapter in my life.

After he retired, he became a public speaker on aviation safety and traveled near and far across the country. As stated earlier, I was fortunate to hear one of his presentations when he was in Colorado Springs in October 1999. He was still traveling and speaking in 2005 when he spoke at the United Airlines Flight Training Center in Denver. His life's trials after the crash continued for him also.

In 1997, his oldest son Tony died in a motorcycle crash. His wife of forty years died two years later after developing a rare infection from a ruptured colon. He nearly suffered another loss in 2002 when his daughter Laurie was diagnosed with aplastic anemia, a rare disease that renders bone marrow unable to make new blood cells. A large amount of money was needed for a bone marrow transplant for Laurie. Insurance would not cover it all. So, Al Haynes sent out a letter to family and friends asking for help, in which hundreds of people who heard of his demise rallied around him to help him save yet one more life. $550,000 dollars was raised.

Another miracle happened, as a young man of twenty-seven donated his marrow. She underwent the transplant and came through ready for a new life. The money raised went to the National Foundation for Transplants, which will cover her transplant-related expenses for the rest of her life. How wonderful that a man who was able to save so many lives was able to save his daughter also, with the help from so many others. Even among adversity and fear, the kindness, hard work, and faith from others does prevail in the end.

Unfortunately, Captain Al Haynes passed on August 25, 2019 at the age of eighty-seven, six days before his eighty-eighth birthday.

Those of us who were aware of his poor health prayed for him and remembered him as we gathered together for the thirtieth anniversary of Flight 232.

32

THIRTIETH ANNIVERSARY

On a hot Friday afternoon, July 19, 2019, a few of the survivors and their families were able to reunite once again at airline attendant Susan White's house in Golden, Colorado, for the thirtieth-year anniversary. Susan had planned this reunion about eight weeks prior and had graciously opened her house to all of us. Channel 4 CBS Denver was there also with their cameras and film crew in order to cover yet another milestone in the Flight 232 story of survival of a major commercial airline crash.

I was excited and apprehensive on the day of the anniversary. I had talked to Rod Vetter earlier that day. He always called me to wish me a happy anniversary and celebrate another year of living. He was unable to attend this anniversary, so I couldn't expect to see him. I was, however, excited to see some of those I hadn't seen since the twenty-fifth anniversary.

A beautiful welcome sign was on the front porch of Susan's house, with some helium balloons attached to it telling us how special we all were and giving every person who entered the front door a special, warm feeling.

Susan and a couple of her close friends smoked a wonderful meal of ribs and salmon. Each of us attending signed up to bring a salad, dish, or dessert. We were not wanting for anything that evening. We had it all—friendship, memories, love, and lots of food!

As soon as we stepped through the front door, Kelly and I were greeted by Susan and asked to fill out a name tag. Survivors were asked to include their seat number on it, and our friend or spouse who came with us were asked to identify themselves with a name tag also. One of the first survivors I saw was my dear friend Garry Priest. We gave each other a big hug—we hadn't seen each other for five years. His mother and sister had accompanied him to the anniversary. I met them years before, but it was still wonderful to see them again. I wasn't familiar with some of the other survivors, but we all still felt like family reuniting after a long absence.

Throughout the evening, we all got caught up with each other's lives and told the story of each of our own survival. What seat we were in, how we exited the burning plane, if we were injured, how long we were in the hospital, and anything else that we could reconnect with. A Sioux City reporter sent their sister station to our reunion to talk with some survivors at the thirty-year anniversary/

reunion. Jeremy Hubbard, local Fox News Anchor, who also covered the twenty-fifth reunion in Sioux City asked if they could come by for about fifteen minutes to take some pictures of the survivors and interview anyone who would like to participate. Throughout their filming, they captured all of us milling around outside in Susan's beautiful backyard. Paul Olivier, who had been the mayor of Palmer Lake in 1989 and had received extensive injuries, shared his story with the film crew. Susan, of course, was interviewed also, as well as a couple of the flight crew who were with us that night.

While we were all seated inside Susan's home, waiting for it to cool off outside, First Officer Bill Records recounted how Captain Haynes instructed him and the flight crew through the intricacies of the plane's mechanics—what to do when one system broke, then another, then another. We were all listening intently to his every word. Those of us attending found out that Captain Haynes was currently in the intensive care unit at a hospital in Seattle. It was with heavy hearts that we realized he would never be able to tell his historic story again. Captain Haynes passed away the next month.

Here is a picture of the fourteen "Thankful Survivors" who were able to gather on the thirtieth anniversary. From left to right (rear row): Tim Owens, flight attendant; Garry Priest, seat 15G. From left to right (middle row): I have to apologize, but I cannot remember the first woman's name that is on the far left. Standing beside her is Ellen Badis, seat 17F; Peter Allen, seat 5E (he was dead heading in first class); Charles Martz, seat 27J; Gary Dean, I am not sure of his seat number; Paul Olivier, seat 33B; Tom Engler, seat 16B; and Bill Records, first officer. Kneeling from left to right: Kathleen Batson, seat 28G; Kathy Tam, flight attendant; Susan White, flight attendant; and myself, Margo Siple, seat 19C.

The director at the Mid-American Museum of Aviation and Transportation contacted Susan regarding an amazing Flight 232 exhibit and would be broadcasting live at 5:30 p.m. our time in Denver. They wanted as many of us who were at the reunion to "like" the page so we could all watch the tour and be able to comment via Facebook as they would be directing the tour specifically for our reunion group in Colorado.

There were a few technical difficulties to start, but we were able to finally receive the video feed from the museum. There had been some additions to the Flight 232 exhibit since the twenty-fifth anniversary when we were there in person.

We were all patiently waiting for the broadcast to begin. Susan White is kneeling as in prayer.

As the special evening wound down, and everybody had had their share of food, some of us left early, including Kelly and myself. I found as many people as I could and gave them all big hugs before we left. Except for those that I keep in close contact with, I am not sure when I will see the familiar faces of our "232 Family" again. I am hoping that we can meet up and see each other and hopefully some additional survivors at least every five years. God willing.

I was later told that a handful of the guests stayed late and closed the night out. I am sure their heads were full of memories and their hearts full of love.

Captain Haynes's funeral was held on October 5, 2019 at New Life Church, Renton Campus, 15711 152nd Ave SE in Renton, Washington. I was not able to attend his funeral, but I was told by a fellow survivor that it honored him as the great man he was before and after the crash of Flight 232, which put him in the spotlight. He left quite a legacy, and I am honored to have known such a remarkable man. Without being the man he was, and with the pride and the professionalism he had during his career as a pilot, I am convinced that not one of us, crew and passengers alike, would have survived the devastating disaster that occurred.

He was the lifeline and patriarch of the whole "232 family." His leadership abilities allowed him to direct his flight crew and all available help that was on the ground during the imminent danger the aircraft was in. In less than an hour, there were 285 rescuers at the ready at the airbase and hundreds more arrived afterward.

He will continue to inspire and astound those who learn about him and the amazing feat he pulled off to bring a 290-ton plane from thirty-seven thousand feet in the air to its final resting place with nothing but manual effort and skill.

Afterword

Currently, after finishing this book, thirty-two years have passed since the day that changed so many lives and taught the aviation industry many lessons and discovered where improvements need to be implemented. I know I have been given an assignment and a purpose in life. I still don't know what these are—I may never know. However, I have been given many blessings and miracles in my life. We all receive them. We just need to recognize them, persevere, and live our lives to the fullest.

The number 232 continues to pop up in my everyday life, even thirty-two years later. One time recently, I had a dream about an airline crash which promptly woke me up. When I looked at the clock on my bedside dresser, it was 2:32 a.m. When randomly opening a book or hymnal while looking for a certain page, it will be page 232 that first appears. A car that was in front of me while in traffic one day had the license plate number FLT232 on it. I later found out that it was a rental car, and the FLT represented the fleet, but the number 232 was boldly staring me in the face. My husband has badge number 232 for membership to a shooting range in southeastern Colorado. We were married years after the crash occurred, and he said that he has always had that badge number. While traveling on any road or highway, I will happen to look at the mile marker and it will be numbered 232. A person's phone number that I have may include 232 in it, or a phone number given on television for a certain add will have 232 in it also. When I first get into the car and turn it on, the time on the digital clock will be 232. When stopping to put gas in the car, the price of gas will be $2.32 a gallon. When Susan White bought meat and other essentials for the thirtieth anniversary BBQ at her house in 2019, she shared and posted a picture of the receipt, which ironically totaled $232 and some odd cents. My daughter has also experienced some of these random occurrences, and she always tells me about them. This is an ongoing occurrence in my life, which I'm sure will continue.

About the Author

Margo Siple is a Littleton, Colorado native. Even though she moved out of state various times since her survival of Flight 232, she has since settled down in Littleton, not far from where she grew up and where her parents still live. She has been an avid reader ever since she learned to read and has always wanted to write and publish a book of her own. She started writing her story twenty-five years ago. After early retirement, she realized she needed to finish her story and encourage others to have faith and persevere against adversity. Margo is also an avid animal lover, especially dogs. A trip to Ireland and staying in a castle is on the top of her bucket list. She enjoys retirement with her husband, Kelly, and they look forward to traveling in the years to come.

CPSIA information can be obtained
at www.ICGtesting.com
Printed in the USA
LVHW070014220322
714057LV00008B/169